The Human Person in God's World

Studies to Commemorate the
Austin Farrer Centenary

Edited by
Douglas Hedley and
Brian Hebblethwaite

D1341357

scm press

© Douglas Hedley and Brian Hebblethwaite 2006

The Authors have asserted their right under the Copyright,
Designs and Patents Act, 1988,
to be identified as the Authors of this Work

British Library Cataloguing in Publication data

A catalogue record for this book is available
from the British Library

Paperback 0 334 04106 6/978 0 334 04106 1
Hardback 0 334 04110 4/978 0 334 04110 8

First published in 2006 by SCM Press
9–17 St Alban's Place,
London N1 0NX

www.scm-canterburypress.co.uk

SCM Press is a division of
SCM-Canterbury Press Ltd

Printed and bound in Great Britain by
MPG Books Ltd, Bodmin, Cornwall

The Human Person in God's World

Contents

Preface and Acknowledgements

Austin Marsden Farrer (1904–68) is regarded by many people as the greatest Anglican theologian of the twentieth century. He exemplified an unparalleled combination of spiritual sensitivity, theological perspicacity and philosophical acuity. In September 2004 a conference on 'The Human Person in God's World' was held at Oriel College, Oxford to commemorate the centenary of Farrer's birth. The conference was inspired – and chaired – by Professor Basil Mitchell, and its success was due, in large measure, to the enthusiasm and hard work of Dr Margaret Yee. About a hundred people, from both sides of the Atlantic, attended the conference. They greatly appreciated encouragement from the Bishop of Oxford, who preached at the Service of Celebration with which the conference ended, as well as the wonderful hospitality and catering of Oriel College.

This book contains, in revised form, the six main papers delivered there. Bishop Harries' sermon is printed as an Appendix.

Special thanks are due to the Alec van Berchem Charitable Trust, the British Academy and the John Templeton Foundation, whose generous support enabled the whole project to go forward.

Douglas Hedley
Brian Hebblethwaite

Contributors

BASIL MITCHELL, Emeritus Fellow of Oriel College, Oxford, formerly Nolloth Professor of the Philosophy of the Christian Religion. His books include *Law, Morality and Religion in a Secular Society*, *The Justification of Religious Belief*, *Morality Religious and Secular*, and *Faith and Criticism*.

NANCEY MURPHY, Professor of Christian Philosophy at Fuller Theological Seminary, Pasadena, California. Her books include *Neuroscience and the Person: Scientific Perspectives on Divine Action* (with R. J. Russell, T. C. Meyering and M. A. Arbib) and *Whatever Happened to the Soul? Scientific and Theological Portraits of Human Nature* (with W. Brown and H. N. Mallory).

EDWARD HENDERSON, Professor of Philosophy, Louisiana State University, Baton Rouge. He has written many articles on Farrer's philosophical theology, and he co-edited (with Brian Hebblethwaite) *Divine Action: Studies Inspired by the Philosophical Theology of Austin Farrer*, and (with David Hein) *Captured by the Crucified: The Practical Theology of Austin Farrer*.

BRIAN HEBBLETHWAITE, Life Fellow of Queens' College, Cambridge, formerly Lecturer in the Philosophy of Religion. His books include *Evil, Suffering, and Religion*, *The Problems of Theology*, *The Christian Hope*, *The Incarnation*, *The Ocean of Truth*, *The Essence of Christianity*, *Ethics and Religion in a Pluralistic Age*, *Philosophical Theology and Christian Doctrine*, and *In Defence of Christianity*.

Contributors

DAVID BROWN, Van Mildert Professor of Divinity in the University of Durham and Canon of Durham Cathedral. His books include *The Divine Trinity, Continental Philosophy and Modern Theology, Tradition and Imagination, Discipleship and Imagination,* and *God and Enchantment of Place.*

DOUGLAS HEDLEY, Fellow of Clare College, Cambridge, Senior Lecturer in the Philosophy of Religion. His books include *Coleridge, Philosophy and Religion* and *The Shaping Spirit of Imagination* (forthcoming).

RICHARD HARRIES (now Lord Harries of Pentregarth), Bishop of Oxford 1987–2006. His books include *The Authority of Divine Love, Christianity and War in a Nuclear Age, C. S. Lewis: The Man and His God, Art and the Beauty of God, The Passion in Art* and *Praying the Eucharist.* Among the books he has edited are *Reinhold Niebuhr and the Issues of our Time* and *The One Genius: Through the Year with Austin Farrer.*

1. Introduction

BASIL MITCHELL

Austin Farrer was born on 11 October 1904. Many will remember him as a man, as a priest, as a teacher and as a friend. In this book he will be considered, rather, as a thinker, in his capacity as a philosopher and a theologian.

In looking back on a thinker of the recent past it is customary to review his achievement and endeavour to place him in the history of his discipline, and indeed to ensure that he has a place in it; to consider what his influence has been and what were the influences upon him; and to estimate which of his ideas deserve to be developed as of lasting importance – as contributing or deserving to contribute to contemporary debate.

These things will, of course, occupy our contributors in due course, but not before attention has been concentrated on the need to understand the thought itself for its own sake and in its own terms. For it has to be admitted that Farrer is a difficult subject for the customary treatment. He was a highly independent thinker, aware of the philosophical and theological controversies of his day, but not allowing his questions or his answers to be determined by them. He was part of no movement and did not initiate a movement. There is no point in trying to compare or contrast him with the other philosophers and theologians of his time. He offers little scope for the journalistic penchant of assigning people to particular centuries or decades of which they are said to be typical. As I said in my memorial address:

He was a man – to use the words of Thomas Traherne – 'as familiar with the ways of God in all ages as with his walk and

I

table'. As such he was an embarrassment to those who were anxious to discern trends and plot correspondences, just as he was, for that matter, to any one making any sort of list; one simply had to name the others, and then to add, 'And then, of course, there was Austin Farrer'.[1]

I must confess to an initial disinclination to any attempt to go beyond Farrer. What he did was so immaculately done that the very idea of improving upon it or developing it can easily seem ridiculous. In the recent history of philosophical theology, he is Bach rather than Beethoven. If his work were to be submerged for eighty to a hundred years, to be discovered by some future Mendelssohn, it would remain a pattern of how Christian philosophy can be done but not one obviously inviting emulation.

Nevertheless, independent thinker though he was, he was deeply rooted in the Oxford of his time. A product of the Honour School of *Literae Humaniores* and the Honour School of Theology, he was thoroughly at home in the language and literature of the Greek and Roman classics and of the early Christian Fathers; and, schooled in the discipline of composing Greek and Latin verses, he found poetry a natural mode of communication with his friends. 'Greats' at that time involved the study of Greek and Latin language and literature, philosophy and ancient history, and thus provided a threefold mental training: in precision of language, clarification of concepts and the weighing of historical evidence. This may have predisposed him to approach the study of the Bible and of Christian theology with the same confident scholarship and critical independence as he would have applied to Plato and Thucydides.

It is an odd fact of cultural history that Oxford produced at that time the remarkable group of so-called 'Oxford Christians' (of whom the best known were C. S. Lewis and J. R. R. Tolkien) whose writing proved to have a universal resonance. Part of the explanation may be that the Oxford of their formative years was, in international terms, something of a backwater, as yet unaffected by the currents which were beginning to enter British intellectual life from the continent of Europe, in particular logical positivism in philosophy and Barthianism in theology.

Introduction

One can scarcely maintain that this state of affairs positively encouraged the development of ideas which were to have a universal appeal, but it can perhaps be said that, if thinkers appeared who had the imaginative gifts to make such an appeal, the setting was such as to favour their creative activity. At a time when the University and its constituent departments had no say in college appointments which were for life, college Fellows had almost unlimited freedom to pursue their own individual interests and to engage in congenial and fruitful alliances. This does not in itself account for the universality of their appeal, but it does in part explain the absence of cultural factors which might have inhibited it.

By the time these factors began to be operative in Oxford, Farrer had already become used to philosophical speculation unrestricted by the narrow boundaries that positivism imposed and to employing reason in theology to an extent and in a manner that neo-orthodoxy forbade. I remember myself complaining when I first met Farrer after World War Two that 'if I listened to the philosophers I could not be a Christian, and if I listened to the theologians, I could not be a philosopher'. (I was not prepared to solve the problem in the manner of Alasdair MacIntyre, then an astonishingly precocious undergraduate at St Mary's College, London, by combining positivism in philosophy with Barthianism in theology. As a logical positivist Alasdair declared theology was nonsense; as a Barthian he replied, 'Yes indeed, the language of theology is meaningful only to faith.')

Given Farrer's originality and independence of fashion it is possible to celebrate his writings as exquisite works of art to be appreciated for their aesthetic qualities alone. In trying to characterize his style I once wrote:

The writing is highly individual, but the personality of the author is in no way obtruded. He is never obscure or involved, but is sometimes elusive. The materials of his thought are so thoroughly fermented in his imagination that no sediment remains (footnotes are notoriously absent) and a sparkling clarity of expression is achieved which can have a certain intoxicating effect.[2]

This style is most conspicuously displayed in his sermons in which he moves from everyday observation by way of philosophical reflection to devotional intensity in no more than fifteen minutes. One is not aware of any shift in language as he passes from one phase to the next.

His philosophical works are no different in this respect. I was recently re-reading *The Road to Xanadu*, that remarkable book in which John Livingston Lowes traces the imaginative process by which Coleridge gathers together elements of his encyclopaedic reading into the imaginative masterpieces of *The Ancient Mariner* and *Kubla Khan*. He has occasion to refer at one point to Berkeley's *Siris*, 'announced as an essay on tar water which beginning with tar ends with the Trinity, the *omne scibile* forming the interspace'.[3]

Farrer resembles Berkeley in being one of those philosophers whose style is an index to his thought; he also resembles Coleridge in that reflection upon the salient features of his style is itself an ingredient in the study of his philosophy. In so far as his style owes much of its distinctiveness to his use of metaphor or, as he liked to say, 'parable', in appreciating his style one is led into involvement with his subject matter. This becomes apparent early in the first chapter of *The Glass of Vision* (which remains my favourite work of Farrer's, perhaps because I heard it delivered as Bampton Lectures in St Mary's in 1948). Having been freed by Spinoza from the belief that God should confront him in some sort of face to face colloquy, he writes:

> I would no longer attempt, with the psalmist, to set God before my face. I would see him as the underlying cause of my thinking, especially of those thoughts in which I tried to think of him. I would dare to hope that sometimes my thought would become diaphanous, so that there should be some perception of the divine cause shining through the created effect, as a deep pool, settling into a clear tranquillity, permits us to see the spring in the bottom of it from which its waters rise. I would dare to hope that through a second cause the First Cause might be felt when the second cause in question was itself a spirit made in the image of the Divine Spirit and perpetually welling up out of his creative act.[4]

A great deal of Farrer's philosophy is set out in this passage and in due course I shall try to indicate what his main contentions are and what problems they raise, as an introduction to the subject matter of this book.

But at this stage, having admitted that Farrer is a writer who can be enjoyed as a stylist and a creative artist, it is worth, I think, anticipating an objection that might be made to our whole enterprise in this book. He was not confronted by the kind of sophisticated postmodernism which is now prevalent, although there had been anticipations of it in Collingwood's 'absolute presuppositions' and Hare's 'bliks'.[5] From this point of view Farrer's philosophical theology represents a powerful and attractive vision of the world, valid and coherent within its own assumptions but not requiring rational assent. In support of this view it could be noted that Farrer himself insists that a Christian philosophy must be lived if it is to be understood and found convincing.

How would Farrer have responded? Some indication is to be found in *Saving Belief* when he considers how we are to decide between theism and pantheism – and this would apply presumably to any other alternative to Christian theism. He asserts that 'we ought not to brush away either the scientific naturalism or the personal realism of western thought as a mere regional idiosyncrasy'.[6] Here he anticipates and rejects the typically postmodernist claim that philosophical viewpoints are culture-bound in the sense that they would only have developed within a given culture and that their meaning and truth-claims are bound up with the basic presuppositions of that culture. It would, I think, have been evident to him that, although, for instance, signal developments in logic and epistemology occurred in fourth-century Athens and could not have occurred in contemporary Sparta, this fact has no bearing on the validity of the actual advances made in these fields. Indeed he makes the point succinctly in *The Freedom of the Will*: 'is it enough to say "because we are conditioned by our culture to do so"? Must we not say, because we are by our culture enabled or set free to do so?'.[7]

Farrer in all his writings remains an out-and-out rationalist. In the preface to *Saving Belief*, an entirely non-technical work,

he asks the question: 'Can reasonable minds still think theo-
logically?' He answers that, for those who make the experiment, discoveries will ensue. But 'these happy discoveries will
come to hand only if we do our religious thinking like honest
men and in one piece with our thinking on other subjects'.[8]
This bold assertion sounds innocent enough, but it runs counter
to one of the cardinal assumptions of twentieth-century analytical philosophy: that only scientific thinking can be deemed
rational.

In his biography of Austin Farrer, *A Hawk among Sparrows*
(a title which has always worried me – Austin was not in the
least predatory and the rest of us were not so inconsiderable: *A
Swift among Swallows* might have been better), Philip Curtis
remarks of Farrer's first visit to America:

> It was good for the Farrers to get out of Oxford into an
> atmosphere in which Austin's enterprises were regarded as
> possible for an intelligent man. There were those in Oxford
> who did appreciate his philosophy and many more who
> appreciated his sermons, but the general tide was against
> him.[9]

Curtis was right in stressing the invigorating effect upon Farrer
of his three visits to the United States. The success of these,
and their lasting effects, are shown by the inclusion of two
essays by American authors in this volume and the presence of
a number of American visitors at the centenary conference in
2004.

That in Oxford the general tide was against him is also
undoubtedly true. It was being strongly asserted by A. J. Ayer
and tacitly assumed by others that metaphysics was impossible
and so, *a fortiori,* was theology. Although logical positivism in
its pristine form was on its way out together with its central
tenet, the verifiability principle, it continued to be assumed that
the paradigm case of reason was afforded by scientific method
and common sense regarded as vestigial science. Philosophers
were discouraged from venturing beyond this narrow perimeter
and were confined to problems which could be treated with
exemplary 'clarity and rigour'.

I have written elsewhere about the effects of this upon me personally:

It is hard to convey the impact upon me of post-war Oxford philosophy. It was severely analytical, and there was a well-nigh universal suspicion of broad questions and comprehensive answers. To someone of my temperament it was bound to appear arid and constricting but to most of my colleagues it was 'the Revolution in Philosophy – a marvellously new and liberating experience'.[10]

It had an obsessional character which tempted its practitioners to behave as if all previous philosophy had been superseded – a tendency nicely brought out in a spoof lecture list which circulated in the later 1940s. It contained the entry: 'Ethics before 1900 – Mr G. J. Warnock (one lecture)'. Warnock's book, *Ethics Since 1900*, had just been published.

The emphasis upon the language of science was to some extent modified by the vogue of 'ordinary language philosophy' which inevitably drew attention to the language of everyday intercourse between human beings. Apart from that it did nothing to enlarge the scope of philosophical thinking.

Fortunately, for the reasons I have already given, it was difficult in Oxford to establish a uniform orthodoxy. A group of philosophers and theologians, of whom Farrer was the central figure, began to meet regularly in 1946 with the common aim of vindicating theology as a rational discipline. They shared with their philosophical colleagues their emphasis on clarity and rigour and a determination to do justice to the arguments of their opponents. Hence Farrer, though not himself a professional philosopher, became familiar with the line they were taking. Although he rejected their limitations, he respected their standards. So when he entered into dialogue with a philosopher, he knew what he was talking about.

Indeed in an important respect Farrer *was* an 'analytical philosopher'. He did not approach philosophical problems with a pre-existing metaphysical theory which he sought to vindicate against rival theories. In a sense he was also an ordinary language philosopher who simply felt entitled to take as his subject matter ordinary Christian language in its doctrinal and devotional use. This Christian language had for him been largely formed by Aquinas, but Farrer was never formally a Thomist, as his friend and colleague, Eric Mascall, was. His project was to take Christian belief as he found it and seek to render it as clear and coherent as he could make it, and relate it intelligibly to whatever else we could claim to know. As he put it in *Faith and Speculation*, where he is discussing the relation between faith and history:

> There is certainly something at stake here and something which calls for philosophical treatment. The issue is not purely philosophical; the theologian will have something to say of the conformity of the one doctrine or the other to the mind of scripture, or its adequacy to the saving effects of revelation. But the theology will be liable to fight a blindfold battle unless the terms of the dispute are philosophically clarified.[11]

Or more concisely: 'philosophy does not create belief; it tests and systematizes it'.

I now return to the question I postponed at an earlier stage, to what extent Farrer's thought is capable of development and represents a model for imitation. So far as his style is concerned it is highly individual and it would be the extremity of bathos to suggest that simplicity and elegance are qualities to be imitated. I take it that no one would recommend for imitation his notorious neglect of such aids to scholarship as footnotes, references and indexes. (One would regard this peculiarity as an indication that he looked upon his books as sketches rather than as finished works, if it were not for the fact that the two that were most thoroughly worked out, *Finite and Infinite* and *The Freedom of the Will*, are no exception in this respect.)

It is characteristic of his approach in his philosophical work that when concentrating on any one problem he is always aware of the bearing of what he is now maintaining on other related problems. In reading him one is always conscious that he is what I like to call an 'epidiascopic' thinker, as distinct from a 'searchlight' thinker. He does not proceed by illuminating now one part of the subject, now another, until he feels he has done enough, but rather, as with an old-fashioned epidiascope, aims to get a large area into clear focus (except that in his case the analogy fails in so far as there do not appear to be occasions when the picture is still fuzzy).

The academic mind is suspicious of epidiascopic thinkers. It is more at home with scholars who address limited problems with accuracy and precision. Their contribution is indispensable, but unless it is balanced by others who look at the whole picture, it is easy for basic assumptions to go unacknowledged and uncriticized.

There are two corollaries of Farrer's procedure, which have permanent relevance. One is that Christian thinkers need to keep in touch with fresh developments in the sciences and the humanities, for it is these which provide the knowledge that theology must accommodate in a coherent statement of faith. That this part of Farrer's programme is worthy of imitation is shown by the excellence and vigour of current work on science and religion as displayed in the work of A. R. Peacocke, John Polkinghorne, Nancey Murphy and others.

The other is that, in the light of developing scientific knowledge, it may be necessary to reinterpret traditional Christian doctrine. Farrer himself in *Love Almighty and Ills Unlimited* had no hesitation in assimilating Darwinism to the traditional account of creation. 'God makes the world make itself' is a principle he applied to the natural world and he took it for granted that the creation stories of Genesis were mythical representations of the way in which God creates and sustains the world. It was entirely consonant with this that he should maintain that these scientific developments had deepened and extended our understanding of the doctrine.

I have vivid recollection of a meeting of the Metaphysicals at which he demythologized the devil, a move which prompted a vigorous retort from Eric Mascall for whom a personal or quasi-personal devil was not dispensable.

It is evident that when there are apparent discrepancies between Christian doctrine and the current findings of the sciences there are different ways of resolving the problem, and Farrer's account of the matter is rendered more convincing by the extent to which current theological controversies presuppose the truth of his basic analysis.

1 One can stand upon the scientific findings as currently formulated and reject any doctrine that is *prima facie* incompatible with them, as Richard Dawkins and Don Cupitt both do. The one rejects religion altogether; the other drastically reinterprets it. One can be an atheist or a radical theologian.

2 One can stick with a traditional interpretation of doctrine as creationists do. One can be a fundamentalist.

3 One can seek to modify either so as to make it compatible with the other. No doubt there are limits to how far this can be done with science, but in the case of Dawkins his account of science may be challenged. As a biologist, it may be argued, he is not very good on physics; and his interpretation of scientific knowledge may be criticized as betraying hidden secularist assumptions of a dogmatic nature. On the side of Christian doctrine the literal reading of Genesis may be charged with failing to recognize the genre into which the book of Genesis falls.

4 One can hold on to the existing interpretation of either in the faith that it will turn out to be true in the long term. Such tenacity is characteristic of scientists as well as of theologians. If in these ways one recognizes an unavoidable tension between holding on to tradition and attempting revision, one is fundamentally a liberal who may incline to the conservative or progressive pole.

Simply to mention these complications serves to draw attention to the centrality of that other concern of Farrer's – the character of reasoning in different disciplines. For by what rational process do we resolve these questions of interpretation? When he asserted that we should 'do our religious thinking like honest men and in one piece with our thinking on other subjects', it seemed a fairly simple contention, but it ran counter to the philosophical consensus of his day. It was also, on the face of it, incompatible with a whole strain of theological reflection which insisted on a sharp dichotomy between divine inspiration and the natural powers of the mind.

At this point we meet once again Farrer's fundamental conviction, expressed in that paragraph in *The Glass of Vision*, that the human mind can become diaphanous – open to the reception of transcendent truth without ceasing to exert its own natural human activity.

There is a delightful etching by Rembrandt of two women teaching a child to walk. The child is at the stage where he is already walking but needs the support of the women to avoid falling down. I don't know if Farrer was familiar with it, but it came to my mind when he claims in *The Glass of Vision* that 'if a child cannot walk unsupported, that is not to say that he is simply dragged and does not walk at all'.[12] This doctrine of dual causation is at the very heart of Farrer's metaphysics and presupposes that the human will is itself free and creative. This explains why he chose to deliver his Gifford Lectures on the ostensibly non-theological subject of the freedom of the will. For unless the human will is free it will not bear the weight of the analogy with the divine will upon which the whole of his metaphysics depends, as he makes clear at the end of *The Freedom of the Will*. The purpose of that book, he says, is 'the work of clearing obstacles from the serious contemplation of any will whatever, whether human or divine; and even, perhaps, of casting some positive light on that human will, from which alone the divine will can be conjectured'.[13]

In Farrer's scheme this dependence of the human on the divine is then extended to include the whole of the created world. To achieve this the analogy has to be considerably stretched. As he puts it: 'The insight we have into our dependence on God is dark, when compared with God's vision of what that dependence is. But it is brightness itself, compared with the fog we are in, over the dependence on God of any physical substance.'[14] As I put it in an earlier essay:

> Farrer liked to operate, in a manner that was not entirely playful, with the notion of a scale of being. We can by an effort of imagination form some idea of what it is to be a dog, and also of what it is to be God. Both are active beings, so to know them is to form some impression of their mode of activity. Farrer became increasingly convinced that this could not be a purely theoretical exercise. Man and dog, God and man, must interact if there is to be understanding.[15]

By this route we come back once again to the issue that surfaced in that passage from *The Glass of Vision* where Farrer speaks of inspiration welling up from a deep spring and also of the dependence of a second cause upon the First Cause. The pool is obviously an image, but is the language of first and second causes analogical too?

This is a problem that Farrer constantly wrestled with. Sometimes he seems to concede that he is bound on occasion to fall back on literal statement. In *Saving Belief*, after a long discussion of the parabolic language of 'God's Kingdom', he concludes: 'if, in a parable, he made men partakers of his kingdom, he will, in a more literal form of statement, make them associate with his Godhead'.[16] However, in *Faith and Speculation* he resists the temptation to say that 'God wills that . . .' is a literal statement. 'To strip away the last rag of analogy, we must say that God simply does will as his creatures will', and that plainly will not do.[17]

My own inclination is to adopt Bishop Berkeley's distinction between 'metaphorical' and 'proper' analogy. He says that by metaphorical analogy God is represented as having a finger or an eye, as angry or grieved; by proper analogy we must understand all those properties to belong to the deity which in themselves simply and as such denote perfection. On second thoughts, perhaps Farrer sees this himself when in *The Glass of Vision* he writes: 'Suppose, for example, I take my will as a symbol of God, because it seems to be a limited instance of something intrinsically infinite, sheer creativity. In such a case the symbolical relation corresponds with a real relation.'[18]

But I must, in these introductory remarks, resist involving myself in the very issues to be treated more fully by the other contributors to this volume. It would have been totally alien to Austin Farrer's conception of his role as a thinker and his practice as a teacher to ask colleagues to confine themselves to the exposition and interpretation of Farrer himself. In the chapters that follow our contributors at the same time develop Farrer's ideas and address the themes he treated in their own independent fashion.

Notes

1 Basil Mitchell, 'Austin Marsden Farrer', in Austin Farrer, *A Celebration of Faith*, London: Hodder and Stoughton 1970, pp. 14–15.
2 'Austin Farrer – the Philosopher', *New Fire*, 7 (1983), p. 456.
3 John Livingston Lowes, *The Road to Xanadu: A Study in the Ways of the Imagination*, London: Constable 1927, p. 310.
4 Austin Farrer, *The Glass of Vision*, London: Dacre Press/A. & C. Black 1948, p. 8.
5 See R. G. Collingwood, *An Essay on Metaphysics*, Oxford: Clarendon Press 1940, and R. M. Hare, 'Theology and Falsification', in Antony Flew and Alasdair MacIntyre (eds), *New Essays in Philosophical Theology*, London: SCM Press 1955, pp. 99–103.
6 Austin Farrer, *Saving Belief: A Discussion of Essentials*, London: Hodder and Stoughton 1964, p. 42.
7 Austin Farrer, *The Freedom of the Will*, London: Adam & Charles Black 1958, p. 285, p. 315.
8 *Saving Belief*, p. 5.
9 Philip Curtis, *A Hawk among Sparrows: A Biography of Austin Farrer*, London: SPCK 1985, pp. 167f.
10 Kelly James Clark (ed.), *Philosophers who Believe: The Spiritual Journeys of 11 Leading Thinkers*, Downers Grove, Ill.: Inter-Varsity Press 1993, p. 40.
11 Austin Farrer, *Faith and Speculation: An Essay in Philosophical Theology*, London: Adam & Charles Black 1967 p. 88.
12 *The Glass of Vision*, p. 32.
13 *The Freedom of the Will*, p. 315.
14 Ibid., p. 314.
15 'Austin Farrer – the Philosopher', p. 454.
16 *Saving Belief*, pp. 99f.
17 *Faith and Speculation*, p. 107.
18 *The Glass of Vision*, p. 94.

2. Downward Causation and *The Freedom of the Will*

NANCEY MURPHY

Introduction

My purpose here is to assess Austin Farrer's Gifford Lectures, published under the title *The Freedom of the Will*.[1] It would be courteous of me to provide a short, pithy overview of the book and a summary of his argument. I have to say, though, that I'm not sure Farrer, were he here today, could do so himself. It is a long book, and could have been improved if it were condensed. Apparently Farrer had some worries that his points might get lost in the forest, and so he added a summary at the end. Unfortunately, the summary is a chapter-by-chapter overview that nowhere gives a synthesis of his own point of view or the structure of an argument.

It may, actually, be unfair to ask for a synopsis of his argument since he says in the Foreword that the book is intended more as an overview of the literature than as a constructive contribution. Noting the number of ingenious papers written on the subject, he disclaimed the ability 'to vie with their detailed thoroughness or formal elegance'. If I were to contribute anything, he says, 'it would have to be by aiming at greater completeness and at a synthesis of topics' (vii).

In my judgement, Farrer came much closer to his goal of completeness than of synthesis. The central thesis of this chapter, however, is that he succeeded far beyond his modest goals in providing a constructive, and I would even say, revolutionary, contribution to the free-will debate. My first goal, then, will be to describe these valuable contributions. I classify these under two headings: first, his anti-Cartesianism and, second, his recognition of what is now referred to as top-down or downward causation – that is, causal influences of higher-level complex systems impinging on their constituent parts. I shall comment on developments in science and philosophy in the past 50 years that confirm the value of these insights, but also provide slight corrections and amplifications of his positions.

While these two contributions together remove a number of *obstacles* to an account of human free will they are not alone sufficient. My next move will be to argue that the recognition of downward causation calls for a radical reframing of the current free-will debate. Contemporary arguments (seemingly interminable arguments) focus on whether or not free will is compatible with determinism. I shall agree with Farrer that determinism *per se* is too vague a target, and emphasize, as he did, the threat of neurobiological determinism. I then argue that the concern with *determinism* here misses the point. The real issue is the threat of neurobiological *reductionism*. Then, if the concept of downward causation has any meaning, the central question is whether humans exercise any downward control over their own neural processes.

In fact, all complex organisms do have control over some of their own parts and processes. The next question, then, is what more needs to be added to this animalian self-direction to constitute what has traditionally been meant by 'free will'. I begin this enquiry with two sorts of resources. One is scientific observations on the distinctiveness of human linguistic abilities, and the capacity language gives us to evaluate our own motives and cognitive strategies. I develop this line of thought further by employing Alasdair MacIntyre's account of moral responsibility. One has the capacity for morally responsible action when one is able to evaluate that which moves one to act in light of a concept of the good.

An important question, then, is whether Farrer would approve of the direction I have taken. While a full study of our agreements and disagreements is beyond the scope of this chapter, I shall point to a number of parallels between his views and my own account.

I end by suggesting that in addition to neurobiology being no threat to free will it also helps us to understand the ways in which we differ from machines and from simpler organisms, such that our behaviour comes more and more to be self-determined rather than merely a product of biology and culture.

In short, I hope to sketch an account of free will that synthesizes Farrer's contributions, but also advances the discussion in light of recent developments in both philosophy and the cognitive-neurosciences.

Against Cartesian materialism

I believe it is Daniel Dennett who coined the term 'Cartesian materialism'. He uses it to refer to the views of brain scientists who have rejected Descartes' dualism but continue to operate with the image of the 'Cartesian theatre': a place or system in the brain where all perceptual and mental activity 'comes together'.[2] My co-author Warren Brown and I have extended the term to cover a variety of other assumptions about the mental and the neurobiological that are holdovers from Descartes' philosophy. These assumptions come into play when one simply substitutes the brain for Descartes' mind. The most obvious consequence is the setting up of a sort of brain–body dualism. Thus, all that is intelligent about us is to be attributed to the brain alone. A subtle form of mind–brain identification occurs when the 'inwardness' of the Cartesian mind is transferred to the brain. Descartes described himself as a thinking thing, distinct from and somehow 'within' his body. Thinking is a process of focusing the mind's eye; but focusing on what? On ideas *in* his mind. Thus there arose the image of the homunculus in the Cartesian theatre, passively receiving impressions from outside and contemplating its own ideas. Another sort of Cartesian assumption is taking abstract reasoning as the paradigm of the mental and then trying to understand emotion and sense perception as degraded versions.

Farrer did an excellent job in the opening chapters of *The Freedom of the Will* of weeding out some of the most pernicious of such assumptions. Here is a witty dialogue with an imagined proponent of Cartesian inwardness: Dick has just received a meaningful communication from Tom. Is it Dick the man or Dick the brain who understands the signal? When we think of the visual organs and the nerves connected to them we are tempted to ask where the signals go. 'All the way in – to where? To where Dick is? But isn't Dick all over himself?' (90). In short, Farrer says, '[i]t is not the brain that thinks or talks, it is the man' (30).

Endorsing Gilbert Ryle's objections to Cartesian accounts of mind, Farrer says that the Cartesian blunder is to think that the proper act of the soul is thought, and that 'the proper form of a statement about the human person is a statement in parallel columns, one about soul and one about body' (16). In contrast, Farrer argues, 'the proper act of soul is heedful bodily action in face of sense perception' (16f.). With this account there is no problem in relating mind to body; the connection between the mental and the physical is already given in the unity of conscious actions, in what Farrer calls 'action-patterns' (52). Thus, conscious bodily behaviour, not abstract thought, should be taken as the clue to the rest of the mental life (19).

Farrer takes up the question of the seat of consciousness. Following his own advice, he begins with the heedful bodily action of a tennis player making a serve. If we ask the phenomenological question of where the player's consciousness is focused, it is not in the brain but in the hand (26); and yet not in the hand alone but in the whole sweep of action (27f.). If we ask the scientific question of the 'seat' of the action, it is in what Farrer calls 'the whole nerve-plant,' which includes the appropriate brain regions but also the nerves of the spinal column and branches reaching all the way to the hand.

To understand abstract thought in light of heedful bodily action, one has to begin with animals' management of their limbs, but then consider the intermediate steps beyond this that have occurred in evolution and are recapitulated in the child's development. First there is development of the vocal organs. After learning to talk without effort, the focus of consciousness is on the content of what is said; we can think aloud. After this, the capacity to think is detached from vocalization (26–30).

Finally, Farrer rejects Descartes' mechanical account of the body. A mechanism is a system composed of inert and separate parts so that when a movement is started the parts move one another in a determined order (51). Living organisms are not mechanisms.

So, to sum up, Farrer rejected the notion that the paradigm of the mental is abstract thought, either *in* the mind or *in* the brain. Rather, the mental is paradigmatically displayed in patterns of conscious bodily action. Descartes' error was 'to start from pure thought, instead of starting from that heedful bodily action, which it presupposes' (316f.).

While Farrer knew that he was on solid ground in his philo-sophical analyses, he was appropriately cautious about the scientific backing of his proposals. He wrote: 'Whether, in fact, our action-pattern is a pure speculation of the philosophical mind, or is a conception with some scientific employment on the borderland of neurology and animal psychology, is a question we leave for those competent to discuss it' (63). In the half-century since Farrer gave his Gifford Lectures, both neuroscience and animal psychology have provided growing confirmation of his 'speculation'.

Although Cartesian materialists still abound in both neuro-science and cognitive science, there is a growing number of those who agree that *mind* is best understood in terms of 'brain and body operating as one in solving real problems in the field of action'.[3] It is obviously impossible to do justice to the literature here, so I shall mention only three contributions, two of which were presented, appropriately, in subsequent Gifford Lectures.

Michael Arbib and Mary Hesse, in their 1983 Gifford Lectures, developed the concept of a *schema*, which is defined as a composable unit of action, thought, and perception.[4] Basic schemas are the simplest building blocks of our cognitive capacities, and include abilities to recognize objects, and to plan and control activities. Our mental life results from the dynamic interaction among many schema-instances. The concept of a schema is meant to serve as a bridge between neuroscience and cognitive science. The simplest of schemas are candidates for description in terms of specific neural networks.

The importance of schema theory in confirming Farrer's insights is the insistence on their action-orientation. Arbib says, for example, that one *perceptual* schema would let you recognise that a large structure is a house; in doing so it might provide strategies for locating the front door. The recognition of the door . . . is not an end in itself – it helps activate, and supplies appropriate inputs to, *motor* schemas for approaching the door and for opening it.[5]

So here is a cognitive science version of Farrer's action-patterns embodied in 'nerve-plants'.

Donald MacKay, in his 1986 Gifford Lectures, made an important contribution in stressing the essential role of feedback from the environment in shaping organisms' behaviour. All organisms act so as to pursue goals, and their action is guided by constant feedback regarding their relative success or failure, leading to re-evaluation of and adjustments to their activity. This calls for an extension of Farrer's concept of an action-pattern. Instead one needs to think in terms of action-feedback-evaluation-action loops.[6] Even single-celled organisms operate in this manner. A protozoan has the ability to register gradients in toxicity in the water in which it swims. If the level of toxicity is decreasing it continues in the same direction; if increasing it changes directions.

A contemporary author, Andy Clark, provides remarkable scientific confirmation of Farrer's central point of view. Clark's book is subtitled 'putting brain, body, and world together again'. Nicholas Humphrey writes that while there have been several revolutions in psychology in its short lifetime, 'no theoretical insight has ever seemed so likely to change the landscape permanently as the one in this brilliant . . . book'.[7]

Clark draws his evidence from disciplines as diverse as robotics, neuroscience, infant development studies, and research on artificial intelligence. His central point is to argue that a version of the old opposition between matter and mind persists in the way we try to study brain and mind while excluding the roles of the rest of the body and the local environment. We need to think of mind primarily as the controller of embodied activity, and this requires abandonment of the dividing lines among perception, cognition, and action. His motto is: minds make motions; mind is always 'on the hoof'.

Clark joins cognitive scientists of other stripes in rejecting a model of neural processing based on formal symbolic thought, but unlike some others does not reject the notion of internal representations altogether. Nor does he downplay the role of language in human thinking. Rather, he emphasizes the ways in which our thinking depends on 'external scaffolding'. One example, as for Farrer, is the observation that we do complicated arithmetical problems with the aid of external props such as paper and pencil or calculators. To the extent that we are able to do mental arithmetic it is because we have internalized these embodied activities.

Clark ends his work with an imagined dialogue that I believe would appeal to Farrer – a dialogue between John and his brain. The brain says, '[a] complex of important misapprehensions centre around the question of the provenance of thoughts. John thinks of me as the point source of the intellectual products he identifies as his thoughts. But, to put it crudely, I do not have John's thoughts. John has John's thoughts . . .'[8]

In short, Farrer was entirely right to speculate that future scientific work would validate the notion of the mental as *essentially* embodied and active in the world.

Downward causation

I move now to Farrer's second major contribution, the notion of top-down or downward causation. Although Farrer himself did not use these terms, there are passages in which he is clearly invoking the idea. He distinguishes between two types of systems. The familiar type is one in which the pattern of the whole is a simple product of the behaviour of its parts. The other sort of system is one in which 'the constituents', he says, 'are caught, and as it were bewitched, by larger patterns of action' (57). As examples he cites the molecular constituents of cells and cells themselves within the animal body. Furthermore, '[n]ew principles of action come into play at successive levels of organisation' (58). Farrer recognizes that he is denying deep-seated reductionist assumptions, but maintains that 'the intransigence of the [reductionistic] physicists . . . need not contradict the claims of the biologists to be studying a pattern of action which does real work at its own level, and leads the minute parts of Nature a dance they would otherwise not tread' (60). In sum, he says:

All we are interested to show is the meaningfulness of the suggestion that a high-level pattern of action may do some real work, and not be reducible to the mass-effect of low-level action on the part of minute constituents. And we are happy if we can show at the same time how the claims to exactitude advanced by minute physics need not stand in the way of our entertaining such a suggestion. (60)

It is unfortunate that Farrer used the metaphors of *bewitchment* and *dancing* in his proposal, as these raise more questions than they answer. In light of subsequent developments of the concept of downward causation it has become possible to give a thoroughly non-mysterious account of the efficacy of higher-level patterns without postulating any interference with physics.

In the 1970s psychologist Roger Sperry and philosopher Donald Campbell both wrote specifically about downward causation. Sperry wrote, for instance, that the reductionist view, according to which all mental functions are determined by neural activity and ultimately by biophysics and biochemistry, has been replaced by the cognitivist paradigm in psychology. On this new account,

[t]he control upward is retained but is claimed not to furnish the whole story. The full explanation requires that one also take into account new, previously non-existent, emergent properties, including the mental, that interact causally at their own higher level and also exert causal control from above downward. The supervenient control exerted by the higher over the lower level properties of a system . . . operates concurrently with the 'micro' control from below upward. Mental states, as emergent properties of brain activity, thus exert downward control over their constituent neuronal events – at the same time that they are being determined by them.[9]

21

On some occasions Sperry wrote, in a manner comparable to Farrer, of the properties of the higher-level entity or system *overpowering* the causal forces of the component entities.[10] The notion of overpowering lower-level causal forces rightly raises worries regarding the compatibility of his account with adequate respect for the basic sciences. In addition, Sperry's use of the concept of *emergent properties* is problematic, in that even today there is no agreed understanding of emergence. Some emergence theses appear to postulate the existence of spooky new entities; others to threaten the integrity of the basic sciences.

Donald Campbell's work has turned out to be much more helpful. Here there is no talk of bewitching or overpowering lower-level causal processes, but instead a thoroughly non-mysterious account of a larger system of causal factors having a *selective* effect on lower-level entities and processes. Campbell's example is the role of natural selection in producing the remarkably efficient jaw structures of worker termites.[11] This example is meant to illustrate four theses, the first two of which give due recognition to bottom-up accounts of causation. First, all processes at the higher levels are restrained by and act in conformity to the laws of lower levels, including the levels of subatomic physics. Second, the achievements at higher levels require for their implementation specific lower-level mechanisms and processes. Explanation is not complete until these micromechanisms have been specified.

The third and fourth theses represent the perspective of downward causation. Third, '[b]iological evolution in its meandering exploration of segments of the universe encounters laws, operating as selective systems, which are not described by the laws of physics and inorganic chemistry'. Finally, fourth:

Where natural selection operates through life and death at a higher level of organisation, the laws of the higher-level selective system determine in part the distribution of lower-level events and substances. Description of an intermediate-level phenomenon is not completed by describing its possibility and implementation in lower-level terms. Its presence, prevalence or distribution (all needed for a complete explanation of biological phenomena) will often require reference to laws at a higher level of organisation as well.[12]

While downward causation is often invoked in current literature in psychology and related fields, it has received little attention in philosophy since Campbell's essay was published in 1974. (I was only aware of this literature through the writings of Arthur Peacocke.) Fortunately, philosopher Robert Van Gulick has recently written on the topic, spelling out in more detail an account based on selection. Van Gulick makes his points about top-down causation in the context of an argument for the nonreducibility of higher-level sciences. The reductionist, he says, will claim that the causal roles associated with special-science classifications are entirely derivative from the causal roles of the underlying physical constituents. Van Gulick replies that the events and objects picked out by the special sciences *are* composites of physical constituents, yet the causal powers of such an object are not determined solely by the physical properties of its constituents and the laws of physics. They are also determined by the *organization* of those constituents within the composite. And it is just such patterns of organization that are picked out by the predicates of the special sciences. These patterns have downward causal efficacy in that they can affect which causal powers of their constituents are activated.

A given physical constituent may have many causal powers, but only some subsets of them will be active in a given situation. The larger context (i.e. the pattern) of which it is a part may affect which of its causal powers get activated . . . Thus the whole is not any simple function of its parts, since the whole at least partially determines what contributions are made by its parts.[13]

Such patterns or entities are stable features of the world, often in spite of variations or exchanges in their underlying physical constituents. Many such patterns are self-sustaining or self-reproducing in the face of perturbing physical forces that might degrade or destroy them (for example DNA patterns). Finally, the selective activation of the causal powers of such a

pattern's parts may in many cases contribute to the mainten-
ance and preservation of the pattern itself. Taken together,
these points illustrate that

> higher-order patterns can have a degree of independence
> from their underlying physical realisations and can exert
> what might be called downward causal influences without
> requiring any objectionable form of emergentism by which
> higher-order properties would alter the underlying laws of
> physics. Higher-order properties act by the *selective activa-
> tion* of physical powers and not by their *alteration*.[14]

Brown and I have developed Van Gulick's account by suggesting a broader range of low-level causal ingredients and by
attempting further to specify the bases upon which selection of
those lower-level factors typically takes place. First the question
of what is selected: Van Gulick says that it is the causal *powers*
of lower-level constituents that are selectively activated. Brown
and I include selection of the lower-level entities themselves. For
example, in Campbell's account, it is the termites themselves,
with their varied genetic materials, that are selected. In addition, it has long been recognized that any causal account
requires specification not only of the laws in operation but also
of the initial or boundary conditions of the system. So, for
example, building a machine involves designing (i.e. selecting a
design for) a physical apparatus in which the relevant natural
laws produce the desired outcome. Fred Dretske has introduced
the very helpful concepts of triggering and structuring causes.
For example, a gas leak is the structuring cause that makes it the
case that striking a match will trigger an explosion. The point of
these examples is to show that downward causation, understood as selection, is entirely compatible with the undisturbed
working of the lower-level laws because the laws themselves
never provide a complete causal account. We always also need
to know the context within which they are operating.

Now, selection *on the basis of* what? I shall be intentionally
vague here: downward causation involves selection on the basis
of how those lower-level entities, processes, structures, *fit into* a
higher-level system. A higher-level system is a broader, more

complex system that incorporates the lower. In this sense, Arthur Peacocke is correct in saying that we are looking at *whole–part* influences. The bases upon which selection is made depend on the sort of higher-level system involved. Features selected *for* include *function, information content,* and *meaning.* For example, characteristics of organisms are selected on the basis of their superiority in serving some function vital to the organism, such as Campbell's termite jaws. I shall come back to selection on the basis of information and meaning in the fifth section below. I shall briefly note in a subsequent section how an account of the downward efficacy of the mental depends on anti-Cartesian insights.

It will be important for my account of free will below that the process of downward selection operates equally well whether the lower-level variants are produced by a deterministic or indeterministic process. In fact, some of the variation over which evolution selects is produced by law-governed processes while many mutations are the product of genuinely random occurrences. So, in general, there are two parts to causal stories of this sort: first, how the variants are produced, and second, the basis upon which and the means by which the selection takes place. A fairly insignificant part of the story is whether the lower-level processes that produce the variants are deterministic or indeterministic.

Implications for the free-will debate

We must now see what ground we have gained in tackling the issue of free will. Much of Farrer's book is structured as a running debate with determinists of various stripes, not always clearly distinguished into categories. He says that his determinist 'changes colour like a chameleon' (vii–viii). I note this lack of clear definition of the enemy not as a criticism. It seems that determinism is a deeply entrenched world-view issue, and when a specific form of it is challenged its defenders tend to shift to other ground. Appropriately, then, Farrer considers arguments from quarters as far removed as psychoanalysis and predestinarian theology.

Farrer's first target is neurobiological determinism, and his work on downward causation and an anti-Cartesian account of mind occur in this context. He seems to have been prescient in giving so much attention to this issue. The recent explosion of neurobiological studies of human cognition has given the worry about neurobiological determinism precedence over others such as social determinism. I shall argue, furthermore, that in the process of addressing this particular issue, Farrer has provided insights that radically refocus the *entire* free-will debate. Here is how Farrer stated the problem:

> Over the whole debate about . . . freedom . . . there hangs the shadow of physical determinism, a theory to which recent work on the brain has given a more definite outline. The functioning of the cerebral cortex is revealed as a system of electrical circuits; and apart from these (it is reasonable to suppose) no human thoughts are thought. Now the functioning of the circuits must presumably be understood physically or mechanically, that is to say, as exemplifying determined uniformities. How then – here is the difficulty – can it plausibly be maintained that an exercise of thought which has its being somehow in the functioning of a mechanical force, is really free?[15]

While the concept of downward causation has scarcely been used in the free-will literature since Farrer wrote, it has become ever more obvious that neuroscience cannot do without it. While human brains have a great deal in common structurally, every individual's is unique. For example, my memory of my grandmother will be realized by means of a different configuration of neural connections than my sister's. The worries often expressed in the media that our thoughts and attitudes are genetically determined is entirely unrealistic. There is nowhere near enough information in the human genome to serve as a fine-scale blueprint for a brain.

Instead, the individual's brain is configured by a dynamic interplay of bottom-up and downward causation. The infant's brain, by means of a process of random growth, develops about three times the number of neural connections it can possibly use. Interaction with the environment selectively reinforces some pathways and neglects others. The ones that are not used weaken and die off. This is a perfect example of downward causation via selection – selection on the basis of function. More particularly, I shall note later, it is selection on the basis of *information content* and *meaning*.

Brain development is strongly dependent on action. As soon as we have organisms with neural systems capable of learning, we have organisms whose action in the environment exerts downward effects resulting in the restructuring of the organism's own neural equipment. This occurs in organisms as simple as fish. The fish's behaviour is not determined solely by the brain nature has given it but also by its own prior interaction with the environment. Human brains are restructured by their action in the natural environment but also, and more importantly, by their interaction with the social environment.

Now, my claim is that recognition of the role of downward causation in restructuring the brain requires a refocusing of the entire free-will debate. Much of the current philosophical literature is structured by the compatibilist–libertarian debate. All agree that if determinism is true, then all human choices are determined by prior causes. Compatibilists argue that determinism may well be true, but it is a conceptual error to suppose that this rules out free will. Libertarians argue that free will requires that our choices, somehow, not be determined. A variety of authors agree that this debate has reached a stalemate. For example, Galen Strawson, in his article on free will in the *Routledge Encyclopedia of Philosophy*, sees little chance of progress in settling this issue: 'The principal positions in the traditional metaphysical debate are clear. No radically new option is likely to emerge after millennia of debate.'[16]

I argue that the insolubility of the problem is, in fact, due to the focus on determinism versus indeterminism. First, as Farrer has shown, determinism in general is too vague to pin down. When we do pin it down in the specific case of neurobiological determinism, we see that determinism itself is not the real issue. The issue, rather, is reductionism – the assumption that the behaviour of the whole is a simple product of the behaviour of its parts. The recognition of downward causation is, essentially, the recognition that there are systems in which the whole has reciprocal causal effects on its parts. And this is true regardless of whether the relevant lower-level processes are deterministic or indeterministic. There is still no consensus on the question of whether brain processes depend significantly on indeterministic quantum-level events. But for addressing the issues of neuro-biological reductionism and free will we do not need to know the answer to this question.

Showing the irrelevance of neurobiological determinism thus involves a shift in world-view. Throughout the modern era it has been common to think in terms of a hierarchy of sciences, from physics through the social sciences, studying ever more complex systems: atoms, molecules, cells, organisms, societies. This is a useful model. But added to it has been the assumption that causation must all be bottom-up, from part to whole. The metaphor of the clockwork universe resulted from combining this assumption with the notion that the laws of physics, the laws governing the smallest components, were deterministic. Thus, the determinism at the bottom level of the hierarchy inevitably works its way to the top.

The development of quantum mechanics and the wide agreement that the most basic laws of physics are indeterministic should long ago have called this picture into question. If we have to *look and see* whether and where the indeterminacy of the bottom level works its way up, we should recognize that we also have to look and see whether and where determinism works its way up. As Farrer noted, we have to ask, of systems at each level, whether they are indeed mechanisms or that 'other kind' of system in which the whole interacts with its parts.

In sum, I have argued that biological reductionism is false. As Farrer recognized, complex organisms are, to a degree, top-down shapers of their own neural processes and structures. Furthermore (while this would require much more extensive argument), I have suggested that this recognition of the very possibility of downward causation defeats the reductionist-determinist assumptions shaping much of the modern world-view, and this, in turn, calls for radical rethinking of the terms of the free-will debate. Notice, though, that the defeat of neuro-biological reductionism does not constitute in itself an adequate defence of free will. It only removes a very significant obstacle. I turn now to consider what more is needed.

Constructing a concept of free will

Simpler organisms pursue goals, that is, they act teleologically. As we have seen, even single-celled organisms have rudimentary capacities to evaluate the outcome of their action and change it when necessary. More sophisticated animals are able to prioritize goals – for example, abandoning the pursuit of food in order to escape a predator. But this does not amount to free will. The task for this section, then, is to ask what more needs to be said about humans in order to defend the claim that they (at least sometimes) act freely. What are the differences between animal cognitive abilities and those of humans that make for the difference between the flexible behaviour and limited self-direction of animals and the genuine free will of mature humans?

Warren Brown and I emphasize two factors. One is the development of symbolic language. The other is what we call self-transcendence, that is, the capacity to make our own behaviour, motives, and cognitive processes the object of evaluation. While lower animals pursue goals pre-set by evolution, humans alone are able to initiate second-order cognitive processes that evaluate and often modify the goals themselves.

Here is a charming and instructive experiment with chimpanzees that illustrates the essential difference. A chimpanzee is given the opportunity to choose between two unequal piles of candy; it always chooses the larger one. Later in the experiment the chimpanzee is allowed to choose, but then the chosen pile is given to a second chimpanzee, and the subject of the experiment gets the smaller one. Children over the age of two catch on quickly and choose the smaller pile. But chimpanzees have a very hard time catching on; they watch in agitated dismay, over and over, as the larger pile of candy is given away. This illustrates the animals' inability to make their own behaviour, their own cognitive strategy, the object of attention and evaluation. Evolutionary biologist Terrence Deacon says that the task poses a difficulty for the chimpanzees because the presence of such a salient reward undermines their ability to stand back from the situation and subjugate their desire to the pragmatic context.

The experiment can be further complicated in a way that begins to hint at the value of language in freeing us from biology. In this phase, the chimpanzees are taught to associate numbers with the piles of candy. When given the chance to select numbers rather than the piles themselves, they quickly learn to choose the number associated with the smaller pile. Deacon says that the symbolic representation helps reduce the power of the stimulus to drive behaviour. He argues that increasing ability to create symbols progressively frees responses from stimulus-driven immediacy.[17]

The capacities for symbolic language and self-transcendence are intimately related. Alasdair MacIntyre's account of this relation is particularly illuminating. In a discussion of the nature of moral responsibility, he describes the capacity for morally responsible action as *the ability to evaluate that which moves one to action in light of a concept of the good*. This requires quite sophisticated language abilities. In order to evaluate a motive for acting, one must be able to formulate sentences complex enough not only to describe the motive, but also to state an evaluation of the motive so described.

Given the close association between the concepts of free will and moral responsibility, it will be instructive to see more of what MacIntyre has to say about cognitive prerequisites for morally responsible action. 'As a practical reasoner,' he says,

> I have to be able to imagine different possible futures *for me*, to imagine myself moving forward from the starting point of the present in different directions. For different or alternative futures present me with different and alternative sets of goods to be achieved, with different possible modes of flourishing. And it is important that I should be able to envisage both nearer and more distant futures and to attach probabilities, even if only in a rough and ready way, to the future results of acting in one way rather than another. For this both knowledge and imagination are necessary.[18]

From MacIntyre's description of morally responsible action, Brown and I extracted the following cognitive components:

1 A symbolic sense of self (as MacIntyre says, the ability to imagine 'different possible futures *for me*').

2 A sense of the narrative unity of life ('to imagine myself moving forward from . . . the present'; 'nearer and more distant futures').

3 The ability to run behavioural scenarios ('imagination') and predict the outcome ('knowledge'; 'attach probabilities . . . to the future results').

4 The ability to evaluate predicted outcomes in light of goals.

5 The ability to evaluate the goals themselves ('alternative sets of goods . . . different possible modes of flourishing') in light of abstract concepts.

6 The ability to act in light of 1 through 5.

Here, now, is the question I want to pose. Does the person who possesses (and employs) the six cognitive and behavioural capacities just listed possess free will? Brown and I answer affirmatively. This is contentious, of course; while the concepts of moral responsibility and free will are closely associated, it is more common in recent literature to take free will as a prerequisite for moral responsibility than its equivalent. I cannot provide an adequate defence of this move here. Note that a major obstacle to such a defence is the fact that there is no agreement on the *meaning* of 'free will'. However, once the clutter of the compatibilist–libertarian debate is sifted out, there are a number of valuable contributions to be found in the long history of the discussion. For example, a major tradition defines free will as being able to act for a reason. There are also various accounts of free will defined as autonomy, and these are distinguished by the authors' perceptions of the greatest threats to human autonomy. One threat, of course, is the threat of external control, but there are also various internal factors such as passions and appetites. A final example: recently Harry Frankfurt has helpfully distinguished first-order and second-order desires, and claimed that we are free when we have the second-order desire to have our own first-order desires. For instance, if I have a desire for revenge, but my higher-order desire is not to have this first-order desire, then I am not free.[19]

Notice that our list of cognitive capacities incorporates

these various ingredients. The central ingredient is self-transcendence, the ability to make oneself the object of observation, reflection, and evaluation. This is what Frankfurt was calling attention to in his recognition of our ability to evaluate our own desires. A second ingredient, of course, is reason – not the mere reasonableness of higher animals, but the ability to enunciate principles against which to judge our own lower-level cognitions and motivations. Regarding autonomy, MacIntyre focuses on development of the ability to form our own moral judgements independent of social conformity – that is, not only the ability to evaluate our motives in light of social norms, but also to evaluate social norms themselves. This is an instance of yet another level of self-transcendence.

Now, an important question is whether Farrer would approve of what I've done. In particular, what would he think of Brown's and my argument that the person with these six capacities thereby has the capacity to act freely? I shall note some parallels in emphasis.

Farrer has a great deal to say about the narrative unity of life. The flick of a wrist is governed by the action pattern (say, a tennis serve) of which it is a part. The choice of words as we write is governed by the memory of what has been said and a vague intention regarding what to say next. Abstracted from one's life history of projects undertaken and values embraced, an act is not so much free as capricious (91, 289ff.).

Farrer endorses the view that to act freely is to be directed by reason (294). He considers the role of imagination and prediction in decision-making. Prior learning will have formed the neural connections subserving a variety of possible actions (41). The neural system, then, produces a readiness for more than one response to a given situation. The agent selects one of these on the basis of predictions of their likely outcome. Both reason and what he calls 'subjective factors' are involved in the selection. Reason will reveal the viability or not of projects that passion recommends; and then the passion, as an effectual motive force, will be suitably modified (283). Equally important, though, is the claim that without the subjective factors of desire, passion, empathy, none of the otherwise reasonable courses of action will be undertaken (283).

Farrer's emphasis on the interconnections among prediction of consequences, evaluation of outcomes, and transformation of goals is summarized in response to an imagined determinist's objection. The determinist agrees that actions are the product of reason and motivation. But motivations are either innate or learned from our culture; reasoning, insofar as it does not go astray, is determined by its own principles. In short, the determinist says, determined reason projects the consequence of a possible action; unchosen appetites and dispositions determine one to act upon it or not. 'And where is the free choice in that?' (295).

In response Farrer objects to driving a wedge between reason and motive or interest. It must be shown that reason does not simply evoke formed appetites and dispositions, but provides 'novel objects in which we freshly interest ourselves' (295). Valuations are *at first* a product of one's culture and circumstances (285), but reason allows us to pass judgement on cultures themselves (284f.).

Here is how Mark Richardson describes Farrer's understanding of self-transcendence in his study of Farrer's Gifford Lectures:

> Farrer claimed that persons have the capacity to invent new principles of action, to be innovative. He returned to this theme frequently in *The Freedom of the Will*, and regarded it as essential to his idea of freedom. By inventiveness, Farrer was referring to the capacities for self-evaluation, holding and assessing collateral beliefs and desires, reflecting upon, and when necessary changing, one's judgements, and adapting to new circumstances by creating new motive principles for action.[20]

So I believe that I am not being unfair to Farrer in claiming that he would endorse the uses to which I have put his writings.

Reconciling neuroscience and free will

Recall that the central problem being addressed here is the worry enunciated by Farrer that the findings of neuroscience conflict with our belief in free will. So far I have addressed the conflict in an abstract way by developing Farrer's insights on downward causation. I want to make a further move in this section, namely to suggest that neuroscientific findings do not only *not* contradict our belief in free will but in fact help us to understand the cognitive capacities that enable free action.

It is not possible to make direct connections between neurobiology and the high-level human abilities that I listed as the prerequisites for free will. Each of these six capacities is complex in itself and requires further analysis into more basic cognitive components before any meaningful connections can be made with neurobiology. Consider just one example, the sense of self. What is at issue here is not the question of what it means to *have* a self. Rather the issue is that of having a self-*concept*.[21] This concept arises early in life, but becomes more complex through maturation.

Developmental psychologist Michael Lewis distinguishes between implicit and explicit self-awareness. The former he refers to as the biological 'machinery of self', the latter as 'the idea of me'. The machinery of self is shared with other organisms; it involves the distinction of self from non-self and conservation of self over time.[22] Patricia Churchland attributes this primitive sense of self to the self-representational capacities of the brain, and lists some of the systems known to be involved – for example, representation of the internal milieu of the viscera via pathways to the brain stem and hypothalamus, and autobiographical events via the medial temporal lobes.[23]

Lewis describes two stages in the origination of explicit self-consciousness. The first is physical self-recognition, which generally appears around eighteen months of age. A more advanced form of self-awareness appears during the third year of life and is measured by the ability to engage in pretend play and also by the use of personal pronouns.[24] It is no accident that use of these pronouns serves as a *measure* of the possession of a self-concept. M. R. Bennett and P. M. S. Hacker point out that to have concepts in general is to know how to use words. 'The idea of me' is thus dependent on the ability to use the words 'I' and 'me'. These words cannot be used correctly without acquisition of a *system* of words including second- and third-person pronouns.[25]

So my claim here is that insofar as the cognitive neurosciences help us to understand the biological bases for cognitive capacities such as self-recognition, they not only fail to threaten our free will but in fact help us to understand *how* we are able progressively to detach our behaviour from both biological and social control. They assist us in seeing the extent to which we are *not* mechanisms determined by our parts.

A caveat is in order here. I have so far said a great deal about the importance of Farrer's insights regarding downward causation. I have not made use of what I have called his anti-Cartesianism, although I have mentioned a few more recent theorists who support his position. These scientists and philosophers argue that mental capacities simply cannot be understood in abstraction from the organism's action in the environment. Language provides an excellent example here. Some say that neuroscience can never explain human language because there is no sense to be made of neural events or structures having *meaning*. I believe that this is correct, *if* one abstracts the neural events from their embodiment and especially from their embeddedness in action. Ryle, Wittgenstein, and Austin argued 50 years ago that language – intentionality, reference, meaning – cannot be understood on the basis of inner *mental* events. By parity of reasoning, language cannot be understood solely or primarily on the basis of inner *brain* events.

If I am correct in my understanding of the nature of downward causation, then there is an intrinsic connection between a post-Cartesian definition of the mental and the demystification of the idea of downward mental causation. It is the embeddedness of brain events in action-feedback loops in the environment that is the key to their mentality. And of course that broader system has causal effects on the brain itself.

Conclusion

It is time to attempt to sum up this overly ambitious chapter. My assignment was to assess Farrer's contribution in his Gifford Lectures and then to carry the discussion further, particularly in dialogue with science. Professor Mitchell has written that Farrer did not think of himself as an original philosopher. My assessment, though, is that he did make an especially important contribution to the problem of free will both by his extension of Ryle's anti-Cartesianism and especially by his sketching out of the idea of downward causation. I argued that these interrelated moves are essential for understanding how biological entities can manifest mentality, responsibility, and free will. In short, human beings are neither mechanisms nor parts inside the body, whether souls or brains. They are complex patterns of activity, with top-down control over some of their own parts and processes.

Notes

1 Austin Farrer, *The Freedom of the Will*, London: Adam & Charles Black 1958. (Parenthetical page references in the text are from the 1966 edition.)

2 Daniel Dennett, *Consciousness Explained*, Boston: Little, Brown, and Co. 1991.

3 Nancey Murphy and Warren S. Brown, *Did My Neurons Make Me Do It?: Philosophical and Neurobiological Perspectives on Moral Responsibility and Free Will* (forthcoming), ch. 5.

4 Michael A. Arbib and Mary B. Hesse, *The Construction of Reality*, Cambridge: Cambridge University Press 1986.

5 Michael A. Arbib, 'Towards a Neuroscience of the Person', in Robert J. Russell, Nancey Murphy, Theo C. Meyering, and Michael A. Arbib (eds), *Neuroscience and the Person: Scientific Perspectives on Divine Action*, Vatican City State: Vatican Observatory 1999, pp. 77–100, 87.

6 Donald M. MacKay, *Behind the Eye*, The Gifford Lectures, 1986, ed. Valerie MacKay, Oxford: Basil Blackwell 1991.

7 Nicholas Humphrey, back cover of Andy Clark, *Being There: Putting Brain, Body, and World Together Again*, Cambridge, MA: MIT Press 1997.

8 Clark, *Being There*, p. 224.

9 Roger W. Sperry, 'Psychology's Mentalist Paradigm and the Religion/Science Tension', *American Psychologist* 43 (1988), pp. 607–13, 609.

10 Roger W. Sperry, *Science and Moral Priority: Merging Mind, Brain, and Human Values*, New York: Columbia University Press 1983, p. 117.

11 Donald T. Campbell, '"Downward Causation" in Hierarchically Organised Biological Systems', in F. J. Ayala and T. Dobzhansky (eds), *Studies in the Philosophy of Biology: Reduction and Related Problems*, Berkeley and Los Angeles: University of California Press 1974, pp. 179–86.

12 Ibid., p. 180.

13 Robert Van Gulick, 'Who's in Charge Here? And Who's Doing All the Work?', in John Heil and Alfred Mele (eds), *Mental Causation*, Oxford: Clarendon Press 1995, pp. 233–56, 251.

14 Ibid., 252.

15 *The Freedom of the Will*, pp. 2f.

16 Galen Strawson, 'Free Will', in Edward Craig (ed.), *Routledge Encyclopedia of Philosophy, Vol. 3*, London and New York: Routledge 1998, pp. 743–53, 749.

17 Terrence W. Deacon, *The Symbolic Species: The Co-evolution of Language and the Brain*, New York: W. W. Norton 1997, pp. 413–15.

18 Alasdair MacIntyre, *Dependent Rational Animals: Why Human Beings Need the Virtues*, London: Duckworth 1999, pp. 74f.

19 Harry Frankfurt, 'Alternate Possibilities and Moral Responsibility', *Journal of Philosophy* 65 (1969), pp. 829–33.

20 W. Mark Richardson, 'Human Action and the Making of a Theist: A Study of Austin Farrer's Gifford Lectures', Graduate Theological Union PhD dissertation, 1991, p. 155.

21 See M. R. Bennett and P. M. S. Hacker, *Philosophical Foundations of Neuroscience*, Oxford: Blackwell 2003, ch. 12: 'As we shall show, the "self" or the "I" (thus conceived) is a fiction generated by conceptual confusions. There is indeed such a thing as self-consciousness in the philosophical sense of the term, but it is not consciousness of a "self". It is a distinctively human capacity for reflexive thought and knowledge, wholly dependent upon possession of language' (p. 324).

22 Michael Lewis, 'The Emergence of Consciousness and Its Role in Human Development', in Joseph LeDoux, Jacek Debiec, and Henry Moss (eds), *The Self: From Soul to Brain* (Annals of the New York Academy of Sciences, vol. 1001), New York: New York Academy of Sciences 2003, pp. 104–33.

23 Patricia S. Churchland, 'Self-Representation in Nervous Systems', *Science*, 296 (2002), pp. 308–10.

24 Lewis, 'The Emergence of Consciousness', pp. 104–33.

25 Bennett and Hacker, *Philosophical Foundations of Neuroscience*, p. 348.

3. Double Agency and the Relation of Persons to God

EDWARD HENDERSON

It is an understatement to say that Austin Farrer offers a rich sense of the relation of persons to God. His overall understanding is a traditional Christian one. Persons are related to God most completely when they respond in faithful and loving obedience to God in Christ and are incorporated thereby into the triune life of God. But Farrer's special contribution lies in the philosophical theory of double agency, a theory he develops in order to understand God's action in the world and to square the belief in God's action in the world with the understanding of natural processes achieved through the mathematical and experimental sciences.

The theory of double agency eliminates the appeal to a God of the gaps, a God who only acts in the world where there is an absence of natural causation. It also eliminates the idea that God can only act in the world by smashing in from outside and momentarily overthrowing or setting aside the natural processes and their usual principles of operation. According to the idea of double agency, God acts instead by acting in the actions of creatures in a way that preserves their natural modes of operation and their integrity as creatures enjoying a being of their own.

The power of Farrer's theory of double agency is that it not only makes philosophical sense of the general idea of divine action in the world but also of the Christian belief in God's special revelation through particular actions. It places such knowledge by special revelatory acts on a spectrum with the more abstract knowledge of God attained through philosophical inquiry and explanation. More than that: the theory of double agency makes sense of the Christian doctrine of the Incarnation.

Basil Mitchell rightly points out that Farrer shares with the liberal theologians of his time a concern to square theology with the scientific world-view and with the methods of natural explanation, the belief that Scripture reflects human limitations and is fallible, and the willingness to subject the doctrines of faith to reasoned reinterpretation in the light of the best understanding and most rational methods of the time. However, throughout the Enlightenment and to the end of Farrer's life and beyond, most efforts to adjust religious understanding to modern modes of thought have turned out to be reductionist – in effect if not in intention. It is an old story. God and human language about God have been reinterpreted in ways that to Farrer's mind emptied out much of their sense.[1] God's reality and the relation of persons to God were interpreted in terms of human attitudes and morality, and the meaning of language about God was reduced to its 'existential meaning' or to its support of moral life. In Farrer's colourful phrase, God and God's action have been reduced to 'the backside of human nature'.[2] Even the insistence that God is the wholly other transcendent reality before whom persons feel absolute dependence or terrifying awe fails to be an affirmation of God's real existence if it does not also include the understanding that God is one in relation to whom persons can act or about whom they are able to do something other than think, speak, or emote. That is, if language about God refers to an existing God, then God must be a God with whom persons can engage.[3]

Farrer's *modus operandi* was to see how far the reasonable person of our time can go toward understanding God as one with whom we can be engaged and toward understanding the practice of orthodox catholic Christianity, that is, of 'mere Christianity', as a way of engaging truly with God. He did this by taking seriously the actual and honest practice of traditional faith in its Anglican expression and pressing its practical understanding as hard as he could, trying not to empty it too quickly of its sense but to find its fullest and richest possible meaning.

This essay offers an explanatory interpretation of Farrer's theory of double agency and applies it first to the idea of special revelation through particular action and then to the belief in the Incarnation. In this way, the explanation and application will clarify the general mode of relation between persons and God and then go on to illuminate the Christian understanding of how the relation can be freely cultivated in the life of faith.

Double agency in the life of faith

Exploring the idea of God's action in the world, *Faith and Speculation* follows the method *Finite and Infinite* used to explore the metaphysical structure of operation in finite entities: let the clearest and most immediately accessible experience in a range of phenomena be the clue to understanding the phenomena that lie at less accessible ends of the range. Now, Christian theists take God's action in the world to be present at all levels of reality. Surely God touches the active being that is the cellular and organic life of persons, but if the working of God's action is open to being experienced directly, then that will be where it engages the self-conscious and intentional action of persons. For Christians, that will be in the life of intentional Christian faith. Assuming the reality of God and of God's activity of creating, sustaining, redeeming, and perfecting the world, we look to see how practitioners of faith might experience the active presence of God in themselves and what that experience reveals about the God–person and God–world relation.

The term 'experience' does not refer to some pure datum given to consciousness prior to the use of interpretative images or concepts.[4] Rather, experience is the consequence in consciousness of an activity of persons in the world, jostling with the multitude of other activities and finding their goal-oriented activity affected or qualified by the beings it runs up against. The activities up against which a person bumps will not be known as they are in themselves but as they affect the interpreting person. The way the knowing person acts and encounters reality will in turn be shaped by the images, concepts, and understanding of what is real, how it works, and what is important in relation to the person's action. Such understanding embedded in practical life makes the knowing person's activity what it is and, consequently, able to know what he or she knows as a result of that activity. That is, in shaping the person's activity, it shapes the way the person interacts with and is affected by the world and thereby the way he or she knows the world. What persons are able to know will depend, therefore, upon the way they act in the world, and the way they act will depend upon those embedded ideas and images that make their action what it is.

So it is with the relation of persons to God. If a person is to know God and God's way of acting in the world, he or she must first act in a way that will allow knowledge of God; that is, the person must act in a way that opens his or her action to affection by God in his or her conscious life as a person. That means living the embedded rationality that makes faith the kind of activity it is. It means taking up the life of faith.

To know a person as a person, one must treat the person as a person. To know God as God, one must treat God as God; that is one must live in faithful relationship with God. If one does so, one can reasonably believe that one encounters God acting within one's own action. Says Farrer, 'We cannot touch God, except by willing the will of God. Then his will takes effect in ours and we know it; not that we manipulate him but that he possesses us.'[5]

The very heart of this experience of faithful obedience is that God acts in the action of faithful persons and that God acts in a way that respects and enhances their freedom and their identity. The experience is that one's act of obedience is not one's own *simpliciter*; it is one's own action and at the same time God's action. Further, the experience is that in this union of actions the person not only remains free but also becomes more truly free and more truly who he or she is. Farrer points to the experience of prayer, which is a self-consciously intentional engagement with God:

> We can, in the only possible way, experience the active relation of a created energy to the Creator's action by embracing

the divine will. Everyone who prays knows that the object of the exercise is a thought or an aspiration or a caring which is no more ours than it is that of God in us . . . We know that the action of a man can be the action of God in him; our religious existence is an experimenting with this relation. Both the divine and the human actions remain real and therefore free in the union between them.[6]

Here we have arrived at the essential and most clarifying experience of double agency. 'Our religious existence is an experimenting with this relation' between persons and God when persons join their wills to God's will. When persons freely choose to join their wills to God they find that their doing so is at the same time a dependence upon God to do in them what they cannot do in themselves. In faithful obedience persons are free, yet they are also submissive to the will of another. They are obedient to the will of another, yet they are thereby most fully in charge of themselves.

The experience of double agency is not the experience of hammer-on-nail force but of two agents co-operating in one action: God acting in and through the person, so that God's action is effective in the person's own action but in a way that lets the person be his or her self and retain his or her identity and integrity. In fact, Farrer claims that in the believer's experience God's action not only respects the person's integrity but also even makes the person more fully who he or she is than he or she could otherwise be.

In the case of intentionally lived faith, there is experience of God's action taking effect in the world and proceeding through double agency. Everything we can know about God's action in the world will be illuminated by the experience of obedient faith, and that experience will have to exercise control over what we can and cannot say about God's action in the world and the relation of persons to God.

We must not think that Farrer is referring us only to our own private experience as the place where we can experience God's action in the world. We will experience it most directly in our own cases. But what we experience in ourselves can also be intelligibly ascribed to and described in others. The description of this experience, in fact, is platitudinous among practitioners of faith. Take the dramatic case of Tattoo Terry.

Terry is a resident in the Louisiana State Penitentiary at Angola, Louisiana.[7] The tattoos that cover him head to toe include a number of skulls with cross bones. These signify killings. For some of these murders he was sentenced some years ago to death, but his sentence was commuted to life in prison without parole when the US Supreme Court ruled that executions as then practised were unconstitutional. For many years Terry mocked the society that imprisoned him and terrified other prisoners with threats of violence and indifference to both their lives and his own. Despite his position of power among the residents, he was open to signs that a different way would bring greater freedom and a better life than the life of violence and intimidation he had long been living. Recommended by the prison chaplain, he agreed to attend a Kairos weekend, which is a programme patterned after the *Spiritual Exercises* of St Ignatius of Loyola and put on in the prison by men from outside (men 'on the street' in the prisoners' parlance). Terry probably attended the programme because he knew it would give him time off from work and because he had heard that there would be food from the outside and an abundance of home-made biscuits. But something happened to Tattoo Terry. Participating in such activities as discussions of life choices and exercises of self-examination, identifying and forgiving enemies, worshipping and singing, while being listened to by men from outside and receiving various expressions of care, Terry began to change. When the weekend was over he stuck with the life discipline it had demonstrated and became active among inmates who encouraged each other in this discipline. In time, Terry became a different man and a leader within the prison, this time not as one commanding fear but as one watching out for others, attentive to them, listening to them, praying with them, and offered them hope for a more meaningful life within the prison. Terry knows that he will never leave Angola alive and that when he dies he will be buried in the prison cemetery on Point Solitude, but he now says that he is happy and free because he knows Jesus and lives with him. He also says that this Terry is the real Terry.

Terry himself says that this transformation is the very work of God, something God has done. The natural processes studied by the physical and human sciences are still there, and one can put Terry's change down to those natural causes alone. But the faithful can reasonably say that it is God at work in Terry, God acting in his actions to make him into the new Terry. He would likely agree with Farrer's statement that persons are not complex single beings but complex double beings: persons acting and God acting in their action to finish their creation.[8]

Terry's transformation does not mean that his life is in every respect more pleasant or that he now will get what he desires. In some ways it is more difficult. He still must spend his days doing uninteresting, even demeaning work. Now he has also to endure the taunts of other prisoners and is not free to retaliate with force. And he must endure the indignities visited upon him by security officers whose own sense of power may be enhanced by reminding inmates that prisoners are nobodies with no power. To the extent that Terry lives the life of faith, he prays for those who misuse him. He resists the urge either to strike back or to defend himself by making himself indifferent and cynical. When he fails to live faithfully, he turns again. And through the failures and the indignities, so far as he manages to stay with the life of faith, he says that because of it he is more free, more himself, and more truly happy than he was before he joined his life to God's by embracing the divine will.

We have been rehearsing platitudes common among actively faithful people. This putative description of double agency as consciously known in free submission to the will of God allows us to make some philosophical observations, which can then be cautiously – we might well say 'agnostically' – generalized to think about God's action at the levels of operation that lie below the personal level.

First, God's action in the obedient faith of persons is not an instance of the co-operative agency of created persons with other created persons. God is the transcendent creator of the world, not one of its created constituents. God is not a member of a class of beings that could possibly have other members. Therefore, the relation of God's action to the action of faithful persons is *sui generis*. In the case of created persons acting in co-operation with each other, we can distinguish the different agents clearly and in principle specify which part of the double action is done by one and which by another and describe or explain the way each created person works. This we cannot do with God.

Critics of the idea of double agency often seem to miss the point about the divine uniqueness. Some demand proof that divine agency is at work in a given case, such as that of Tattoo Terry, and hold that our inability to give the proof is a disproof of God and God's action in the creature. Others claim that there is, in fact, hard proof that certain effects could not possibly have a natural explanation and must, therefore, be the work of God (as, for example, in the case of putative miracles as violations or suspensions of natural processes). But either to demand or to offer proof that God's action is responsible for specifiable and predictable worldly effects is to think that God's action is subject to the same kind of proof, description, and manipulation as are the activities and interactions of created things. It is to reduce God to a natural constituent of the world.

The uniqueness of God also refutes the objection that it is logically impossible for free human action to have both a human and a divine agent. Human freedom in divine–human double agency would only be logically impossible if God's action were a form of created action. Then they might be incompatible just as being a triangle is incompatible with being a square. On the contrary, we know that the double agency of God and human persons is possible because we can think it and experience it.[9]

The transcendence of God and the uniqueness of God's relation to the world are also related to two closely related and mutually illuminating points that Farrer makes about double agency. One is that we cannot locate the causal joint, the other that what we experience is always the *effect* of God's action and never the process or mechanism by which God enacts the effect.

Take the point about the causal joint first. That we cannot locate it means that because God is God and we are not, we can never specify precisely where and when God's action enters the world in relation to a particular human action, or say where God's action leaves off and the person's action begins. Thus, we may rightly say that Tattoo Terry's new life is something God is doing, but we cannot say that God's action first entered the process during the Kairos weekend. That may be the time when Terry intentionally engaged with God and became conscious of God's active presence; but Terry himself may recognize a multiplicity of ways in which God's action was already at work before his response; for example, in his mother's prayers, in his own dissatisfactions about his life, and in his natural intelligence as one able to understand the language and practices of faith to which he is introduced.

The action of God in Terry's faith includes the general action whereby God establishes and preserves the world in being and in being the kind of world in which free personal agents can live and act. But it also includes the special action of God in the Incarnation, for that is the action of God to which Terry has chosen to attach himself. And it may involve a further special action whereby God's action engages with Terry's to give the latter understanding, strength, and direction.

That we cannot locate the causal joint between God's action and ours does not mean that there is none. If we are to affirm God's special actions, actions in which God undertakes new things and is not restricted only to making the world follow certain repetitive structures, then we must think with John Polkinghorne and others about features of the world or places in it that are open to God's action. Farrer certainly affirms this. Indeed, in choosing the act of embracing God's will as the place where persons most directly experience God's action, he identifies a certain feature of personal existence as a place of openness to God's action.

A second point about double agency is that what one experiences in the act of joining one's will to God's is one's action as an *effect* of God's action. One does not thereby gain access to the 'inner' life of God whereby God does what God does. God's inner life is in principle hidden from us. This should not be scandalous to the philosopher. If God is God and the *sui generis* reason why there is a world and why it is the kind of world it is, then we cannot hope to bring God down onto our own level, laying God's active being beside our own, so that we can clearly describe the inner workings of both agencies and define their similarities and differences as we can the agencies of two created persons.

Following Farrer's method of illuminating less accessible phenomena by taking the most accessible as a clue, we adopt a stance of necessary caution and principled agnosticism about those levels of divine activity prior to and below the personal level. Everything we dare to say about God's action in nature and in history must be said in awareness of the inescapable limits of human access to God. So Farrer says little other than that God makes the world to make itself and acts in it by respecting rather than overthrowing the natures of things, waiting on creatures and responding to them rather than forcing them either by imposing a rigid plan upon them or by smashing the structures of the order God has nurtured into being.

The double agency theory is hospitable to the effort to locate 'places' of the world's openness to divine action. Polkinghorne's idea of the sensitivity of chaotic systems to top-down causality understood as 'energy inputs' or 'information inputs' is certainly consistent with Farrer's understanding of God's action in the world.[10] But speaking of such inputs does not, for the reasons explained above, amount to a locating of the causal joint between divine and creaturely action. Farrer acknowledged that the causal structure of the created order is sufficiently loose as to allow God's action, as it were, to enter and initiate new effects and trains of consequences following from them, just as it is sufficiently loose to allow free human action within it. Polkinghorne's own words acknowledge and almost quote Farrer: 'The causal net of the universe is not drawn so tight', he says, 'as to exclude [the] possibility that God interacts with the history of his creation by means of "information input" into its open physical process.'[11]

The double agency theory is also hospitable to the idea of top-down causation as discussed by Nancey Murphy in her chapter in this volume. Indeed, the idea of top-down causation has roots in Farrer's exploration of the mind–body relation in *The Freedom of the Will*.[12] Murphy's work toward establishing the viability of this kind of causation as operative in human action supports the analogical use of the idea in understanding God's action in creatures. In fact, insofar as top-down causation is a theory especially applicable to understanding the mind–body relation and the free agency of persons, it fits with Farrer's analogical use of the mind–body relation in understanding God's action in the world as double agency.

The top-down action of persons through their bodies gives us an example of creaturely double agency. One of the creatures is the human body with its skeleton, musculature, organs, and nervous system, the other the thoughtful person whose body it is. These are distinguishable but not separable. When a person thoughtfully decides to perform an action, the decision in no way overthrows or forces bodily action against its nature. Rather the free and conscious agent decides and acts, and the body responds. That is what bodies properly do. Effort may be required, but the body does what bodies are naturally able to do by being what they are. What the body does can be described in purely bodily terms. The body is itself, even in being directed by a decision. Suppose, for example, someone waves an arm. We can understand the waving in physiological and neurological terms. Yet that understanding will not be complete if the waving is done by a person acting consciously and purposefully. We will not understand the waving without understanding what purpose it is intended for. Does it mean 'hello', 'go away', 'look at me', or 'watch out'? Thus, there is the person and there is the person's body, two distinguishable constituents of the world. The decision of the person to wave takes effect in the body without cancelling the body's nature as a body or going against the grain of its nature.

Analogously, Farrer says, God 'acts as the soul of the world'.[13] God achieves God's purposes in the world by acting in the world without smashing its natural order. This, again, is not an explanation of what goes on 'within' God when God acts to produce a worldly effect; it just says that it is reasonable to believe that God does it. Just as we can freely make bodily movements without understanding or being able to explain how our decisions take effect in our bodies, so God can surely act in the operations of the constituents of the world without our being able to explain God's own life.

Suppose, then, that we say that God acts in the world by a top-down information input analogous to the top-down causation involved in deliberate human action. We will not thereby have moved beyond the use of images to a knowledge of God's action as it is in and to God, and we will not have located the causal joint between God's action and creaturely processes. If we identify information that structures the world as an effect of God's action, the term 'information' may be taken quite literally. However, that term does not give us a description of the action whereby God inputs the information. If we try to think about it, we will find ourselves thinking of God as, for example, a cosmic computer operator or, perhaps, as a cosmic story writer, a cosmic playwright, or the soul of the world. These may be true and useful images if we recognize that they are not literal descriptions of God's very own life and agency. What they do tell us is that however God does it, God's agency gets organization into the finite agencies that constitute the world in a way that does not overthrow them but lets them be themselves.

Special revelation as proper knowing

Knowledge by revelation is often thought to by-pass the processes through which we acquire ordinary knowledge of the world around us, a kind of knowing such that its content is, as it were, 'zapped' into our minds, given in a way that has no intelligible connection with our ordinary, natural, and rational ways of knowing. Double agency, on the other hand, lets us see knowledge by revelation and knowledge by reason differently.

Whatever we know of God we know through the interpretation of God's effects. This is true both of God's action in creating and sustaining the world as the kind of world it is and in the particular actions that constitute special revelation. The action of creating and ordering we may call God's general action; the existence and order of the world, God's general effects. The action of creating and ordering is particular enough. But we call it general because its effects are the existence and common structure and ways of operating that are found everywhere. On the other hand, we call the things God does in particular times, places, and creatures but not in all, God's particular or special actions. In both cases, what we know are divine effects, and these are all operations of creatures.

General and particular knowledge of God is analogous to general and particular knowledge of human persons. We know human agents by the way in which we interact with the activity in which they have their being. Because we experience their active presence, we know that persons exist. Because we observe them in groups, on the whole and in the main, we know that they behave in regular ways. The social sciences apply their methods to the study of such behaviour. Their methods of observation are ways of acting in relation to persons. Because the interaction is of the kind that focuses on common characteristics that lie over the whole face of human behaviour, it yields knowledge of a general and abstract nature. It tells us how people of certain types in certain conditions can be expected usually to act, but it does not tell us how a particular person is going to act or what his or her peculiar character is. It does not give intimate knowledge of individual persons as friends, colleagues, or enemies.

On the other hand, because we interact with individual persons in activities other than observing and looking for common characteristics, we come to know some of them more concretely and fully than social scientific study allows. We come to know them as individuals with unique characters. This more determinate knowledge of individuals also comes through interacting with persons in certain ways but in ways different from the interactions that studies the general forms of behaviour. We think of the general sort of knowledge as more scientific and rational than the more individual sort, but both are proper ways of knowing and both are, in fact, appropriately rational. It would not be rational to try to know someone as a friend by putting them through a series of psychological tests in order to characterize their behaviour according to defined types. The two kinds of knowledge have in common that they derive from and are rooted in ways of interacting with their objects. If the way of acting in relation to someone is appropriate to the kind of relationship one seeks to have with the person, then the knowledge one acquires will be proper and rational.

Applying the analogy, we can say that there are these same

ways of knowing God. One is more general and abstract, the other more particular and concrete. Looking at the most common features of all creatures, the facts that they exist at all and operate according to common principles and structures, we may conclude that existence and order are effects of God. We will then say that we know by reason that God is the source of the world's existence and general character. But in a meaningful sense, we could also say that these general characteristics of God are revealed, for anything that is the effect of action reveals or discloses the will and character of the agent.

Christian theists believe, however, that God's action is not limited to what God does to establish and sustain the general order of things. Believing that God can and does act in particular ways at particular times and places and in particular persons – a belief the theory of double agency renders intelligible – they interpret certain events in the world as the effects of God's particular or special action. It is not hard to generate a list of some of those that have special significance in the history of Christian faith: the calling of Abraham, the appearance to Moses, the Exodus, the giving of the Law and establishment of the Covenant at Mount Sinai, the inspiration of the prophets, and the whole complex of events that constitute the life, death, and resurrection of Jesus. These all reflect events and human actions that allow interpretation as effects of God's action. Such particular events are limited to particular times and places and can be experienced only by those who are, so to speak, in the right place at the right time, though they can be recognized, reported, interpreted, and communicated by others. Some such events have become the foundation of sacramental rites. Thereby the events are repeated so that others can participate in them. Such cases reveal God in more particular and concrete ways than do the general features of the world, yet the particular action of God becomes generally available to humankind through them. In sacramental co-operation with the grace that is God's action, persons gain a richer and more intimate knowledge of who God is than is possible from the discovery of the common features of reality that reveal God to philosophical inquiry. Yet in both kinds of experience, God reveals his character by what he does. Persons come to know not only that God is creator and orderer of the world, but that God is one who desires communion with them, who has expectations of them, who commands, loves, redeems, and sanctifies them. Creeds, canons, and confessions formalize as doctrines such discoveries about who God is and what God is doing. Faithful persons say that they have come thereby to know God not only as the creator of heaven and earth but also as the Father Almighty. They say also that they have come to know Jesus of Nazareth as the eternally begotten Son and the Holy Spirit as God enlivening the faithful with divine life, and so on.

The knowledge of Jesus of Nazareth as the Incarnation of the Eternal Son of God is like the knowledge of a friend or of a person with whom one works closely. Although the kind of knowledge provided by the social sciences may have value in our relations with other persons, we do not get our knowledge of friends as friends from psychology. We get it from doing with them the kinds of things friends do with friends. We get it from treating them as friends or living in relation to them as friend to friend. In an analogous way we may come to know the active presence of God in Jesus of Nazareth only by acting in the way that makes such knowledge possible. That action is the complex action of loving, trusting, and dependent obedience that constitutes life as a life of faith. It means seeking the will of God in the ways that are provided: searching the Scriptures, participating in the sacraments, praying, worshipping, and, most importantly, actively loving one's neighbours. It is reasonable for those who do so to believe that they encounter God's action qualifying their own, as an action that they run up against and know as effective in their own. And, indeed, if God does act in particular ways, it is only reasonable to think that one will know the effects of those actions and what they signify of God if one acts in the appropriate, the faithful, way. Thus, the knowledge of God by special revelation is not some utterly unintelligible phenomenon but is a proper form of human knowing on a scale with the philosophical knowledge of God through the recognition of God's general effects.

The Incarnation as double agency

If we grant that it is reasonable to believe that God has indeed acted in Jesus, does that justify understanding the action in terms of the traditional doctrine of the Incarnation? Indeed, does the idea of the Incarnation make sense? The theory of double agency shows that it does.

The doctrine that Jesus is both divine and human has been widely criticized as irrational. If Jesus is divine, the criticism goes, then he could not but know as God knows and do as God does. And in that case, he cannot be a human being who struggles with real choices and makes free decisions on the basis of incomplete knowledge and faulty understanding. Instead, he must be a supernatural person in whom God miraculously, unilaterally, and coercively cancels out the human limits. Since those limits are part and parcel of being human and since Jesus does not have them, he cannot truly be human. But if we go the other direction and insist on Jesus' real humanity by affirming that he struggles as we do to live his life with all the limits of human knowledge and human power, we remove the differences between Jesus and ourselves whereby we call him divine. Thus we get Jesus as a great man, a hero of faith, but not divine.

To overcome the criticism and to show that the affirmation of Jesus' humanity and divinity is a reasonable articulation of the encounter with Jesus we must explain first how double agency lets us affirm Jesus' real humanity. Then we must explain how double agency lets us affirm his divinity consistently with the affirmation of his humanity.

If the Incarnation is a matter of double agency, then it means that God's action in Jesus is not so completely different from God's actions in other persons that the two have no common ground. To put it positively, God's action in Jesus is coherent with God's action in other persons: both are by double agency. The Incarnation is not an incoherent surd. Furthermore, inasmuch as we have experience of non-coercive causation among creatures, we need not regard Incarnation as a unilateral coercion of the man Jesus, so that Jesus in fact has no integrity, freedom, or reality as a man.

The scale of double agency

It is not enough to put Jesus' humanity and divinity in coherent relationship with the being of other persons. We must also clarify the difference between God's action in Jesus of Nazareth and God's action in other persons. We can clarify that difference by deploying the idea of double agency in two ways: first, by imagining and applying a scale of double agency and, second, by distinguishing different intentions of God.

What is meant by a scale of double agency? In *Finite and Infinite* Farrer spoke of the 'scale of operations' we experience in ourselves. At the highest end of the scale are self-conscious acts of deliberate decision-making. In such acts we know what we are doing in doing it. But not all our actions are as open to consciousness as acts of deliberate decision. Below them will be self-conscious activities performed pursuant to decisions made without a process of deliberation, then others performed in an unthinking satisfaction of appetite. Further down the scale will be activities of habit and activities that are unconscious, yet still able to be made conscious and, therefore, rightly called 'personal'. As we go down the scale, the interior structure of the activities and their relation to our freedom as persons becomes less and less clear.

Similarly, then, we can think of a scale of double agency. We place different creaturely activities at different places on the scale according to the degree of closeness and mutual interpenetration we see God's action to have in them. Farrer himself suggests such a scale: 'the relation between the underlying act of God', he says, and the created energy overlaid upon it, is not everywhere the same relation.

In the case of mere physical forces, there is the highest degree of mutual externality between the two; it is natural enough to speak of God's action here as the action of a cause. In the case of rational creatures, there is more mutual penetration; the entry of the divine into the human may be called inspiration on the one side, and co-operation on the other. In the person of Christ the mutual interpenetration is complete; it is necessary to talk of a personal identity.[14]

How many points are there on the scale? In this passage Farrer distinguishes but three: mere physical forces, rational creatures, and the person of Christ. All overlap in that Christ is a rational creature, in fact a human person, and in that all rational creatures rest upon and depend upon lower level physical operations. By locating Christ at the apex of the scale, we use the idea of double agency to bring him and God's relation to him into intelligible relation with other creatures and God's relation to them. But we do so in a way that recognizes the difference between Christ and every other force, entity, organism, or person on the scale. In Jesus, the Christ, we say that God's action and the man's action are perfectly united. What Jesus does is what God does in Jesus. What God does in Jesus is what Jesus does. In our own case we know our actions to be by varying degrees at odds with God's will; nevertheless, we can speak of God's acting within us insofar as we grasp divine purpose and co-operate with it. In physical forces, where the operations are unable to intend co-operation with God's will, God's action is more like that of an external cause. Consequently, while seeing God's action in all created operations, we also recognize that God acts differently in different creatures and in different kinds of creatures. In Jesus God achieves a perfect unity with humankind.

If we assert so thorough a union of God's action with Jesus' action, however, may we not be implying that Jesus is not truly a human person like us, that his humanity is supernaturally possessed, coerced, cancelled? Not if we use the scale of double agency. The possible interpenetration of God's action with the action of creatures increases as we move up the scale from merely physical forces to rational creatures. The greater the interpenetration of divine and creaturely agency, the greater the freedom and individual integrity. As we have already seen in describing the experience of faith: the more our actions conform to God's will, the more God's actions enter into ours and the freer and more truly ourselves we are. If we see Jesus to be at the topmost point on the scale, then we must surely say that if God acts so completely in Jesus' actions that what Jesus does is what God does, Jesus is supremely free and supremely himself. Neither his real humanity nor his particular personal identity are forced and cancelled by divine action. They are set free and fulfilled. In Farrer's words:

> We see that the increase of divine penetration into creaturely action does not remove, but enhances, the freedom of the creature. And so, without pretending to see the mystery of his being from the inside, we must believe that Jesus is both more human and more fully himself than any man.[15]

To say that in Jesus we reach the apex of the scale is to say that Jesus' union with God's action is the highest possible degree. To say that it is the highest possible degree is to say that in this case God realizes a uniquely important action. Though God's action in Jesus may be on a scale with ours and intelligible to us in terms of double agency, God's relation to Jesus' life is not the same as God's relation to the acts that constitute our lives. In the case of Jesus we are provoked to say that 'in the person of Christ . . . it is necessary to talk of a personal identity'.

We must be careful in stressing the identity of Jesus with God not to commit the common mistake of dropping off his real humanity or of making it seem, as many in fact do, that Jesus only appears to be human. To avoid that mistake, Farrer insists that we see Jesus 'as a Galilean villager of the first century' who so used the 'Jewish ideas he inherited' as 'to be the Son of God'.[16] We should not see him as one the content of whose mind was identical with that of the omniscient creator's. Nor should we think he thought of himself in the terms of the creeds. Jesus was very much a man of his time whose mind was formed by his Jewish parents and by the rabbis to whom he listened. What matters is the use he made of the knowledge he received. And that, says Farrer, was a divinely perfect use.

> It became in his head the alphabet of ideas through which the spirit within him spelt out the truth of what he was, and what he had to do. He was not saved from factual errors in matters irrelevant: he was not prevented from supposing that Moses wrote the whole Pentateuch, or that the world had begun five thousand years ago. But he saw in detail day by day with an

unerring eye how to be a true Son to his Father, and a true saviour of his people. He walked in factual darkness by spiritual light; where knowledge was not available, love and candour steered him through. He never judged wrong on the evidence he had; he discerned between good and evil, and marked us out the path of life. He started, like the rest of us, from nowhere – from a germ in the womb; he found the whole truth, through death and resurrection.[17]

Saying, then, that God acts in Jesus differently from the way God acts in us, because in Jesus he acts to make his Eternal Son incarnate, does not entail that Jesus' real humanity is but a sham. As long as we think concretely about the real humanity, the theory of double agency lets us say that both the divine and human natures are present in one person, neither excluding the other.

God's particular intentions in his action that is Jesus

The doctrine of Incarnation tells us more about the relation of God's action to our action than that Christ's action is perfectly united with – may we not say 'embedded in' – God's action. For we can recognize the distinct content and intention of God's action in Christ as numerically and substantially different from God's action in other faithful persons – in St Peter, say, or in a 'model village carpenter'.[18]

What places different acts of obedient faith at different places on the scale of double agency is the degree to which the act and the life composed of such acts is open and obedient to the divine will generally. But Jesus' life is not distinguished from ours only by virtue of his obedience in loving God and neighbour. Many lives in which one loves God and neighbour are possible. Jesus could have lived such a life, Farrer suggests in *Saving Belief*, 'by remaining a model village carpenter all his days, and dying a natural death at a ripe age' (74f.). But Christians have claimed to see in Jesus' life more of God's action than that. They have claimed to see God's action of salvation for the world:

the very action of Jesus is divine action – it is what God does about the salvation of the world. In the common case of a good human life, humanity supplies the pattern and God the grace. In Jesus, divine redemptive action supplies the pattern, and manhood the medium or instrument. A good man helped by Grace may do human things divinely; Christ did divine things humanly. (75)

Farrer's point here is that the action God does in Jesus is a different action, that it has a different intention and content, from God's action in other persons. What God does in the life, crucifixion, and resurrection of Jesus Christ is a particular action. That it is is unremarkable. All actions are particular and are distinguishable by their content and circumstances. Surely we can speak of God's having different intentions for and doing different things in different people at different times, places, and circumstances. Even if other persons succeeded as did Jesus in being perfectly attuned to the divine intention for them, and even if they were wholly successful in carrying them out, what God intends and what the action of God would thereby accomplish in their actions would be different from the intention God accomplishes in Christ's actions.

God acts in Moses to deliver the Children of Israel from bondage in ancient Egypt and to form a covenant with them under the terms of the Decalogue. God acts in Deutero-Isaiah to bring about a new understanding of the Covenant. God acts in Abraham Lincoln to end slavery in the United States. God acts in Martin Luther King, Jr to eliminate the Jim Crow laws that unconstitutionally continued slavery. And, to take two more ordinary cases, God acts in the village carpenter, who lives to be a good provider for his family by making good cabinets and doing his duty for family and society, and God acts in Tattoo Terry to enable him to make a meaningful life for himself and to help others do the same in the dreadful circumstances of prison life.

In all these cases the intentions and the actions of the person performing them have their various roles and scopes. So far as they are all instances in which God makes the creatures make themselves, they belong to one single and all-inclusive perfect act of love whereby God creates, redeems, and sanctifies. For God's actions are one action in that all are pursuant to the eternal divine intention that defines the nature or character of God. Yet God's actions are many in that God has created and is engaged with a multiplicity of distinct entities, some of which are free and all of which comprise a world whose exact course is open and unpredictable. Different ones of these creatures are related to different divine intentions within the one all-encompassing intention. What is peculiar about God's action in Jesus, say orthodox Christians, is that in Jesus, God fulfils the universal and eternal intention of divine love to redeem the world. In Jesus, God does 'what God does about the salvation of the world' (75).

God's actions in other creatures are not unrelated to this intention, for the same intention of love is fundamentally at work throughout God's creating and relating to the world. Some lives and events, those running from Abraham through Moses, the Exodus, and the prophets, for example, may have a clearer relation to divine redemption than others, though even in this sacred history we see mixtures of motives, confusions of purpose, and failures of faith. In them, God's action appears to us 'as a persuasion of our mixed and foolish aims' (73) toward an end not clearly seen or unconditionally seized. We see these same mixtures, confusion, and failures in the lives of those who lived in contact with Jesus in his time and place – in his followers, the crowds, the established religious people, the officials of government. And we see them also in ourselves and in the lives of all who came after him, both inside and outside the scope of Christendom. But in the ministry, crucifixion, and resurrection of Jesus of Nazareth, says Farrer, 'the natural medium – that is to say, the human story – loses all its opaqueness; the life of Christ no more stands between our perception and the action of God, than the lenses of a telescope stand between us and the star on which it focuses' (74). Seeing the difference we judge its meaning: 'The life and person of Jesus is achievement as perfectly divine as it is perfectly human' (73), 'the very action of Jesus is divine action – it is what God does about the salvation of the world' (75).

Traditional Christianity specifies the particular action of God in Jesus yet more fully by saying that Jesus is the incarnate Son of God. Why? Because Jesus' life is seen to be the expression within the conditions of human existence of the active love that God is. That is, what we see in Jesus is not divine substance put together with human substance as though two incompatible kinds of metaphysical 'stuff' were emulsified into one thing, but the living out in human terms of a perfect and continuous act of love received and love returned. Jesus' life, death, and resurrection are not imperfect images or hints at divine love; they are its clear and present reality. They are love so received that it makes Jesus all that he is and love so returned that it shows Jesus' love to be all that the giver gives and is.

What we see in Jesus is identical with the love that constitutes the very life of God-in-God. When we see this we see that it is right to say that Jesus is not simply the God-who-was-man,[19] but the expression in a particular man, who lived in particular conditions, of the active knowing-loving-doing that is God, the one who is all he wills to be and who wills to be all he is.

It would be impossible for God to live the life of God whereby God is God and the creator of the world and at the same time and in the same respect live that life within the world God has created:

> God cannot live an identically godlike life in eternity and in a human story. But the divine Son can make an identical response to his Father, whether in the love of the blessed Trinity or in the fulfilment of an earthly ministry. All the conditions of action are different on the two levels; the filial response is one.[20]

Farrer goes on to say how the action is different within the life of God in God and within the life of God in the world.

> Above, the appropriate response is a co-operation in sovereignty and an interchange of eternal joys. Then the Son gives back to the Father all that the Father is. Below, in the incarnate life, the appropriate response is an obedience to inspiration, a waiting for direction, an acceptance of suffering, a rectitude of choice, a resistance to temptation, a willingness to die.[21]

These conditions and the forms of action relative to them are familiar to us. They are the very conditions that define the field in which our own lives of faith must operate. 'For such things are the stuff of our existence; and it was in this very stuff that Christ worked out the theme of heavenly sonship, proving himself on earth the very thing he was in heaven; that is, a continuous perfect act of filial love.'[22]

How is it that such an Incarnation of the Eternal Son is the act whereby God redeems the world? By the Incarnation, God communicates who God is, announces God's desires for persons to become part of that same divine life of love, and makes it plainly accessible to them. By faithfully receiving and obediently returning the love God expresses in Jesus, persons participate in the life of divine love. God acts in the actions of persons to the extent that they open themselves to receive the divine grace by trying to discern and obey the divine will. They become 'children' of God. Their lives – that is to say, the actions by which they are themselves – become embedded in the very life of God, which is the will that they embrace.

This rhapsodic articulation of Christian theology has carried us a long way from the usual fare of philosophy. Nevertheless, insofar as this rich interpretation of the man, Jesus of Nazareth, is one that takes his life as something God has done, as an effect of God's action in the action of the man, it places our knowledge of him in continuity with our knowledge of other divine effects. If it is reasonable to see the transformation of Tattoo Terry as something God has done, then it is reasonable, too, to go up the scale of double agency and to see the story of Jesus of Nazareth as the story of what God has done to save the world. Thus we see the revealed doctrine of the Incarnation as continuous with our natural knowledge of the world.

We do not, indeed, know the revelation of God in Christ in exactly the same way that we know God is the transcendent creator of the world. The latter we know by reading the existence and nature of the world, facts generally accessible to all, as effects of God's action. The former we know only by hearing and responding in faithful life to the story of the particular person, Jesus of Nazareth. But in both cases we read worldly events and features as effects of God's action. Therefore, the recognition of God in Christ is not utterly discontinuous with the recognition of God in the existence and shape of the world.

Conclusion

How are persons related to God? God's action comes first and is always present and at work. Persons, then, are related to God by the pervasive and prior presence in them and in the world around them of the creating, redeeming, and perfecting action of God. In this sense persons are related to God in the same way as are rocks, paper clips, electrons, and horses. But because God's action has brought our active existence to the personal level of knowing and aspiring free agency, we persons can also be related to God by consciously recognizing and intentionally embracing the divine will. Doing so joins persons to the prior and greater action of God and makes them participants in the divine life, with hope for the fulfilment of a union that transcends any experience of it we are able to have in this life but to which our aspiration as knowing, loving, and acting persons points. Christians dare to see in Jesus of Nazareth God's action of relating to humankind in a way that most clearly shows them what the divine will is and offers them a way to embrace it by sinking their wills into the will that is the life of God, thereby joining their lives to that life. Unhappily, there is another side to the opportunity of persons to join themselves to God. They may also act contrary to the divine will. They may fail to see what it is and what it requires of them. Or, if they have seen it, they may nevertheless reject it and choose their own opposed ways. For our part, we are bound to believe that God's will does not cease to will the inclusion of all, however much some may set themselves against it.

That Farrer's thought about God and God's action in the world as double agency has shown itself to be fruitful for Christian theology will not necessarily recommend it to those who do not already take traditional Christian belief seriously. But the non-Christian should recognize that seeing Jesus' life as the fulfilment of God's redemptive work does not commit the orthodox Christian to saying that only those persons are related positively to God who know and think in terms of the credal statements of these truths or are baptized into the Church that asserts and preserves them. Insofar as the lives and actions of persons receive and return God's active love as their ways of understanding, their religions, their cultures make possible, they, too, participate in and are freely related to God. No doubt, they will understand their lives in other than Christian terms. They may not in any sense understand themselves as responding to the will of God known through the effects of God in the world. Yet their lives may well effectively if unknowingly or on other terms place their action within what Christians will see as the action of God. Such is the point of the parable of the sheep and the goats (Matthew 25.31–46). The Christian will know from the Christian standpoint that the Way, the Truth, and the Life have found them, and they will understand and live their relation to God by joining themselves to Christ as the incarnate Son of God.

Notes

1 See Farrer's sermon, 'Emptying Out the Sense', in Austin Farrer, *A Celebration of Faith*, London: Hodder & Stoughton 1970, pp. 31–5.

2 Austin Farrer, *Faith and Speculation*, London: A. & C. Black 1967, p. 8.

3 See Farrer's discussion of this theme in chapters 2 and 3 of *Faith and Speculation*.

4 Farrer rejects the idea of pure and uninterpreted experience, also of cognitively meaningful thought with no roots in active experience. See *Faith and Speculation*, chapters 1 and 2.

5 Austin Farrer, *A Science of God?*, London: Geoffrey Bles Ltd 1966, 107.

6 *Faith and Speculation*, 66.

7 The name is fictitious in order to protect the privacy of the real person. However, it is a name of the sort residents of prisons are inclined to give each other. Kairos International is an interdenominational ministry to prisoners inspired by the *Spiritual Exercises* of St Ignatius of Loyola. Its objective is to form the residents into Christian support communities following a rule of life within the prison. The Louisiana State Penitentiary at Angola is commonly called simply 'Angola'. It was originally an 18,000 acre plantation worked by slaves from Angola in Africa; hence the name. After the War Between the States, the plantation became a prison. Through the years it has had a reputation for being a dreadful place where

prisoners were horribly mistreated. It has changed drastically in recent years. Although 70 to 75 per cent of the prisoners are serving life sentences (most without the possibility of parole), it is now possible for a prisoner to make a meaningful life with some dignity. Some believe that the transformation of Angola (but the changes could be reversed on very short notice!) is due to the involvement of such programmes as Kairos.

8 See Farrer's sermon, 'The Burning Glass', in Austin Farrer, *Said or Sung: An Arrangement of Homily and Verse*, London: The Faith Press 1960, pp. 106–11.

9 But two agents for one action is not impossible for all cases of created agents. See 'The God Who Undertakes Us' in *Captured by the Crucified* (eds David Hein and Edward Henderson), Edinburgh: T & T Clark 2004, for examples. See also Tom Settle, 'The Dressage Ring and the Ballroom', *Facets of Faith and Science, Volume 4. Interpreting God's Action in the World*, Ancaster, Ontario: The Pascal Centre for Advanced Studies in Faith and Science 1996. There are many, many examples of such co-operative agency, actions that realize their goals not by the coercion of one by the other but by the mutual co-operation of two or many more agents.

10 John Polkinghorne, *Quarks, Chaos and Christianity*, New York; Crossroad 1994, pp. 69, 71.

11 Ibid., p. 71.

12 Austin Farrer, *The Freedom of the Will*, London: A. & C. Black 1958. The term 'mind–body' relation must not be supposed to imply metaphysical dualism. Farrer denied that mind and body are two kinds of substance. Instead, each is a mode or combination of modes of operation. Throughout his life, from *Finite and Infinite* to *Faith and Speculation*, Farrer held the metaphysical position that to be is to operate.

13 *A Science of God?*, p. 85.

14 Austin Farrer, *Saving Belief*, London: Hodder & Stoughton 1964, p. 75.

15 Ibid., p. 79.

16 Ibid., p. 80.

17 Austin Farrer, 'Incarnation', in Austin Farrer, *The Brink of Mystery*, London: SPCK 1976, pp. 19–21.

18 *Saving Belief*, p. 74.

19 See Austin Farrer, 'Christ is God', in *Said or Sung*, pp. 89–94.

20 *The Brink of Mystery*, p. 20.

21 Ibid.

22 Ibid.

4. God and the World as Known to Science

BRIAN HEBBLETHWAITE

Readers of the best-selling book on punctuation, *Eats, Shoots & Leaves*,[1] might be inclined to think that a comma is missing from the title of this chapter. Its subject matter is certainly not scientific knowledge about God and the world. The chapter's title should really be 'God, and the World as Known to Science'; for I do not have in mind such broad uses of the word 'science' as in 'theological science' – to quote T. F. Torrance's title[2] – or indeed in Farrer's own *A Science of God?* (although the question mark at the end of Farrer's title must not be forgotten). What I want to explore here, in the light of Farrer's work, is the relation between the world as known to the natural (and human) sciences and the God who made that world and acts within it by providence and grace.

I begin by summarizing Farrer's understanding of the difference and the relation between the approaches of the natural (and human) sciences to the world and the approaches of religion and theology to the world. Throughout his writing life, Farrer had a clear picture both of the difference and of the relation between these approaches. In a short piece in the journal *Illuminatio* for 1947, reprinted as the prologue to *Interpretation and Belief*, he observed that 'science obtains precision by artificially limiting its subject matter'.[3] He made the same point in *The Glass of Vision*, published the following year: the information yielded by instruments – physical or conceptual – is real, but selective, relative to the yardsticks we use.[4]

This point is stressed and developed in the two books with which I am especially concerned here. In *A Science of God?* Farrer stresses again the selectivity of the sciences.[5] They use a variety of sieves for selecting those aspects of reality to be studied (in physics, for example, the measurable action of forces on forces). Theology, by contrast, tries to see things in depth and in the round. It does not ignore the results of scientific research, but it concentrates on their relation to God and on what God creatively and providentially brings about in and through them. In *Love Almighty and Ills Unlimited*, Farrer insists that, while science concentrates on the rules and uniformities exemplified by natural forces, theology focuses on the God who makes individuals in and through these natural forces.[6] But, for Farrer, the hand of God is perfectly hidden. The line between natural tendency and divine direction cannot be seen by us, precisely because, as Farrer puts it in *A Science of God?*, God is not a part of the world, still less an aspect of it.[7] That is why nothing that is said about God, however truly, can be a statement belonging to any of the sciences.

In *The Glass of Vision*, Farrer acknowledges that the theologian respects the facts disclosed in the natural and the human sciences, but insists that these are only aspects or dimensions of reality. Respect for the being of things, *a fortiori* for the being of persons, makes the scientist more than a scientist, it makes him a metaphysician. 'That is only another way of saying', Farrer rather nicely adds, 'that as well as being a scientist, he is a man; and, indeed, most scientists are human beings.'[8] The metaphysician – and the theologian is, of course, a metaphysician – does not ignore science, but his prime interest is humane philosophy. Already, in *Finite and Infinite*, Farrer had observed that what makes the typical metaphysician is a balance of scientific and moral passion. (He added a highly pertinent footnote about Kant in this connection: 'If in Kant the two were liable to come unstuck, that is an index of his ill-success.'[9])

The limits of scientific knowledge, therefore, are transcended in personal knowledge and in moral knowledge. In a broadcast review of Gabriel Marcel's Gifford Lectures, reprinted in *Reflective Faith*,[10] Farrer again contrasts scientific truth, experimentally verified and conformable to laws, with moral and personal truth, which requires deep penetration into the very being of a particular individual person and of particular persons in relation. Such personal knowledge comes first and foremost through personal interaction. But the same is true of decision and choice. In *The Freedom of the Will*, Farrer points out how a scientific account of a decision, reducing it to factors and causality, as he puts it, is not an account of a decision at all, but only of events in which the decision took shape.[11]

A fortiori, God's action transcends both the natural and the human worlds. As Farrer says in his introduction to Leibniz's *Theodicy*, again reprinted in *Reflective Faith*, 'God's action cannot be a factor among factors; the Creator works through and in all creaturely action.' We can never say 'this is the creature and that is God' of distinguishable causalities in the natural world.[12] Divine transcendence, therefore, is not just a higher degree of transcendence than human personal and moral transcendence. It is a different kind of transcendence altogether. For the human person remains a part of nature and a product of nature even when, in the spheres of morality, personal existence, and interpersonal relation, we transcend the world of nature as studied in the sciences. God's transcendence is in no way part or product of nature. On the contrary, the world of nature and the human world that has emerged from it are products of God's agency and the sphere of God's action from a wholly other dimension. Nevertheless it is human will and human agency that supply the primary analogies for our talk of God's will and God's agency.

Later in this chapter I shall be returning to the question how God's providential action takes place in and through creaturely energies and agencies. But my primary concern now is to stay at the creaturely level and examine not so much the moral and personal transcendence of human persons, but rather the way in which, notwithstanding that transcendence, human persons are rooted and grounded in the natural world explored by science, and, moreover, necessarily so. Indeed my main purpose is to defend and explore that necessity. Here I shall be developing the idea that finite persons are necessarily fashioned in and through an evolving material world.

But, first, I consider not so much the necessity as the fact of our rootedness in nature. That human beings are embedded in the natural world and are products of biological evolution goes without saying. We are a highly developed animal species. Our higher powers of thought and action are inextricably bound up with our physicality and our senses. Consciousness begins with sense; and personal life, as Farrer puts it, is incarnate in the reactors of the brain.[13] In *The Freedom of the Will* he spells out the way in which the mind organizes patterns of behaviour and action at lower levels – the latter being instrumental to the efficacy of the former.[14] In *Saving Belief* he dwells on the complexity of these levels – atomic, molecular, cellular, vegetable, animal, social – and on the amazing way in which God makes the higher forms make themselves in and through their interaction. 'Science studies the pattern', he says, 'but theology assigns the cause'.[15] He emphasizes the point, to be developed in much greater detail in *A Science of God?*, as we shall see, that it takes the whole story of evolution to make any one of us.

> Were we not remarking that if God wished to make no more than any single one of us, he would need to make half a universe? And why? Because no one of us would be the creature he is, if a thousand thousand lines of converging history, both physical and personal, had not met in him. Your life or mine is but a half-sentence in the book of the world. Tear it from its place, and it cannot be read; or if it can be read, it signifies nothing.[16]

The 'need to make half a universe' is, of course, a typical instance of Farrer's rhetoric. In fact, what he had said earlier on was 'For you to be what you are involves a universe.'[17]

Already, this factual rootedness of the higher forms of personal life in the action and being of lower forms involves a kind of necessity. If God wished to make any one of us, he would *need* to make half a universe. This goes both for the long evolutionary and historical narrative that lies behind each person's formation, and for the organizational hierarchy of levels just mentioned. The very nature of our personal sensitivities and of our rational and creative capacities and potentialities is bound up with the underlying structures that they organize and utilize.

In a word, both the history and the structure are internal to the values of personal life that they make possible and that they embody.

This kind of necessity, reflecting factual conditions internal to the realities and values that are made possible by them and that supervene upon them, is precisely the kind of necessity explored and defended by Saul Kripke.[18] In *Naming and Necessity*, Kripke, by distinguishing necessity from analyticity, is able to show convincingly that certain properties are essential to objects and states of affairs being what they are – objects and states of affairs that, in themselves, are wholly empirical. I think Farrer and Kripke would have been in agreement about this kind of essentialism. It is far from necessary that there should be human beings. But human beings, if there are to be such, are necessarily formed in and through evolution, history, and particular life stories of nurture and growth.

One implication of this kind of essentialism is that Bertrand Russell's remark, in *The Analysis of Mind*, that 'there is no logical impossibility in the hypothesis that the world sprang into being five minutes ago, exactly as it then was, with a population that "remembered" a wholly unreal past'[19] cannot possibly be accepted. For 'human beings' posited in being five minutes ago with built-in 'memory' traces would not be human beings. The suggestion is logically incoherent, if we take logic to include factual necessities as well as analytic ones. The point being made by both Farrer and Kripke is that a real history of formation and growth, and a real history of interpersonal relation are internal to what it is to be a human being.

Similar considerations enable us to reject the notion of middle knowledge (*scientia media*) as a possible divine attribute. I will not discuss here the question of God's alleged knowledge of counterfactuals of freedom, except to say that the tenability of that notion depends on the coherence of compatibilism. Farrer convincingly refuted that idea in *The Freedom of the Will*. But middle knowledge requires not only a compatibilist account of free will and determinism; it requires also the coherence of the idea that God could just actualize a world containing only those free creatures who, God knew, would act well – God's middle knowledge enabling him to make that selection. But a world of particular persons cannot possibly be actualized just like that, even by omnipotence. If some such rootedness in nature and some such history of formation and growth in and through relations with others as we find, factually, to be the case, are essential to our being the persons we are, then it is incoherent to suggest that fully formed individuals could just be actualized – or indeed that a specific process of formation leading to just this or that individual could just be actualized. The point is similar to the point made against Russell. For us to be the persons we are, there has to have been an open, evolving, universe, a complex history of the formation of cultures and societies, and actual life histories of free persons in relation.

Before turning to the implications of all this for theodicy, I want to dwell on the other side of Farrer's treatment of what it is to be a person. I have been stressing our rootedness in nature, but what have been drawn out of nature are spiritual beings, persons made in the image of God. As Farrer puts it in *Love Almighty and Ills Unlimited*, man shares the good and evil of animal – physical – nature. But 'he is a talking beast, and in his speech lies his reason. Through reason he shares, however faintly, that truth which is the mind of God, and becomes a copy or reflection of the divine likeness, in short, a person.'[20] And, in *A Science of God?*, he writes: 'The most godlike thing God creates is a person.'[21] Farrer points out again that sub-human nature, including our own, already has a plus – a creative pull or persuasion leading to higher forms. In persons the plus is much greater: they can enter into the creative thoughts of God and further his purposes by doing his will. Man reveals God in serving as a sketch and as a pencil, Farrer concludes. Made in God's image, he becomes God's instrument.[22]

I now turn to the implications of our necessary rootedness in nature for theodicy. The fact that the very existence of human life and of all the values of human life are inextricably rooted in nature and bound up with all the law-governed dimensions of nature and society that science researches enables Farrer and ourselves to sketch the first stages of a viable theodicy, not only in respect of the free-will defence, but also in respect of natural evil – the side of the theodicy problem on which Farrer concentrates in *Love Almighty and Ills Unlimited*. For it is the same law-governed energies and forces that make us and all the sensitivities and values of our human being possible that also render us vulnerable to clashes and accidents and deprivations of often horrendous kinds. As with all animals, our own exposure to disastrous accident is a function of our physicality.

It follows that accidents and disasters cannot be thought of as having been planned, arranged, or sent by the creator. Let me quote Farrer at some length here, since the point is of some significance in countering popular misconceptions about creation and providence.

> It was for the best . . . that God made a half chaos of self-moving, brainless forces to be the bottom and soil of his creation, out of which higher forms could arise. But then a semichaos, if it is to be itself, must be a field of limitless accident; and accident is by definition an uncalculated effect. It may be foreseen, provided against, discounted, or profited by; it cannot be intended or arranged. It would be meaningless to say that God himself planned the detail of a chaos, or of a semichaos either, in its chaotic aspect. His infinite contrivance draws some good out of every cross-accident . . . But he has not calculated the accident with a view to the resultant good. If he had, it would not be an accident, it would only seem to be one.[23]

The apparent austerity of this aspect of Farrer's theodicy is mitigated by two factors, first by the factor just mentioned, namely, God's ability to bring good out of evil in innumerable ways, and, second – and this is really the supreme instance of the first point – God's promise of eternal life for his finite personal creatures thus arduously fashioned here below. Farrer was quite clear that the costs of our formation in and though the physical universe would be unacceptably high if we could not hold to the Church's conviction of a perfected consummation of all things in the ultimate future, a consummation in which life's personal, human, victims, will all share.

I wish to concentrate for a moment on one aspect of our rootedness in physicality that raises very acute problems for theodicy, namely, the death of infants and the fate of imbeciles. Farrer devoted a short and highly controversial appendix in *Love Almighty and Ills Unlimited* to this problem, under the title 'Imperfect Lives'.[24] He suggests there that it is a function of our animality that some human births just fail to reach the stature of humanity, the stature, that is, of being a rational person (or a speaking and loving person, as he also puts it). With such cases there is not yet, and with total imbeciles there is never, a creature capable of being immortalized by our creator and redeemer. Farrer is sure that God 'loves and saves whatever is there to be saved or loved' and that 'if there ever was a speaking and loving person, there is a creature for God to immortalize'. 'But if the reasoning person never developed, what are we to think? The baby smiled before it died. Will God bestow immortality on a smile?'[25]

Farrer's many critics over this appendix were probably unaware that the Farrers themselves had experience of handicap in their own family. But, of course, handicap is something very different from infant death or total imbecility. We may still wonder about Farrer's emphasis on language and reason as necessary conditions of a fully human stature. But the issue of when personhood begins is a very acute one, not least in respect of the ethics of abortion. Farrer himself writes:

> Shall we say that every human birth, however imperfect, is the germ of a personality, and God will give it an eternal future? We shall still have to ask why the fact of being born should be allowed a decisive importance; we shall wonder what to think of children dying in the womb, or suffering abortion; and we shall be at a loss where to draw the line. Not that it will be any easier to draw it if we equate the origin of an immortal soul with the attainment of speech or reason. For we shall still have to ask, What degree of reason? Rationality comes by stages in those who acquire it, and not all imbeciles are totally mindless.[26]

This is indeed a problem, and one could imagine Farrer's arguments being called upon to justify not only abortion but also infanticide. Peter Singer, for example, now attempts to justify infanticide, not for Nazi-like eugenic reasons, of course, but on utilitarian grounds for putting the most severely damaged out of their misery, as we do with animals.[27] Farrer himself would certainly not have approved of that. Of such cases, he writes, 'Out of natural piety, and a respect for the divine image in man, we treat them as human. We do not kill our imbeciles; we baptise dying infants, and give them Christian burial.'[28] But, all the same, it is clear that he did not think that they were really already immortalizable persons.

I have myself a grievous personal interest to declare at this point; for our first child was discovered, in the twentieth week of pregnancy, to have ceased to grow, since, by then, as it became clear, there was a total lack of amniotic fluid. On urgent medical advice, the foetus had to be aborted for the mother's future's sake. I recall holding this dead half-formed foetus in my hands, perfectly formed from head to waist, then tapering away to nothing. Against all canon law and, I dare say, against all reason, I baptized the child Leslie, my own middle name – and also since its sex could not be determined at the time and the name could be spelled either way. Later, we were told that it would have been a boy. After all the medical research had been done, the body was returned to us in a tiny coffin, and we buried him, with a short religious ceremony, in our Suffolk churchyard. But do I really think that there was, already, an immortalizable child of God in that tiny form? Following Farrer, I think I have to say no; or at least all I can say, with Farrer, is that the matter is wholly in God's hands.

These considerations do have a bearing on the ethics of abortion. It seems wise, indeed imperative, to draw the undrawable line at viability, and, just because of scientific progress, to halve the legal age for permissible abortions, permissible for genuinely medical reasons. And the use of embryos up to 14 days for IVF or medical research does seem defensible, ethically speaking. For we cannot seriously suppose that these embryos are already immortal souls destined for heaven, any more than are the millions of fertilized eggs that do not implant and are naturally washed away. Fourteen days is, admittedly, an arbitrary figure. But, as Peter Geach once argued, if you want to build a house and are unsure where the firm ground ends and the marshy ground begins, you build the house well back of the uncertain terrain.

I now come to the most central and important theodicy question. Granted that specifically human life is essentially bound up with its physical roots, both in terms of its evolutionary background and in terms of its many-levelled structure, did the creation of finite personal life have to be like this? Is there a deeper necessity for some such grounding, some such formation from below, some such drawing of God's personal creatures out of nature into spirit?

Farrer, at times, shows considerable diffidence over the supposition that we can answer this deeper question why. In *Saving Belief* he writes:

If it be asked why a Providence which mends the world did not make it such as to need no mending, we answer that the question conceals and involves another question, Why God made this world rather than some other; and this second question is one which we neither need ask nor indeed are able to ask.[29]

On the other hand, a little earlier in the same book Farrer rejects categorically the notion that we can imagine a world of persons fashioned some other way than by rooting them in, and drawing them out of, a physical universe of law-governed energies and forces that can and do at the same time cause so much harm. 'You suggest that God might have made some such higher forms as he has made without rooting them in the action and being of lower forms', he writes, 'I reply that we have no power to conceive anything of the kind.'[30] And in *Love Almighty and Ills Unlimited* he not only toys with, but actually endorses, the idea that some such rooting is necessary.

Let us examine the way in which Farrer does this in his theodicy book. In the chapter on 'Physical Accident',[31] with many caveats about our ability to answer the question why God has made the world as he has made it, he nevertheless goes on to sketch two highly anthropomorphic parables which do propose at least an indirect answer to this question. The first we may dub an Augustinian parable, namely the parable of the gardener who chooses to plant inferior beds when the superior are full. Thus God may be thought of as deciding 'to invent a further and lower level of creatures when each higher level is complete'.[32] Now we must be quite clear that Farrer explicitly rejects this parable. Unlike the gardener's limited field of activity, infinite inventiveness cannot be thought bound to move to a lower level, when any kind is exhausted. 'What logical reason is there' Farrer asks, 'against an indefinably great number [of kinds], all different, and all of equal nobility?'[33]

Having rejected the Augustinian parable, Farrer tries a different approach, sketching what, with John Hick, we may dub an Irenaean parable, indicating why the creator has to begin from below. In order to have finite personal creatures, with a being and nature of their own, the creator has to place a kind of screen between his infinite glory and their creaturely selves. The material, evolving, universe is just such a screen, begun with the most elementary organization of energy, and gradually built up, level by level, till rational personal beings emerge, thoroughly rooted and grounded in what is fundamentally other than God.[34]

Farrer ends this chapter with a return to diffidence about our ability to handle such deeper questions why. All the same, there is no doubt about his preference for the second, Irenaean, parable, even if he allows an element of the Augustinian parable to stand, namely, its insistence on the value of each level of creation in itself. But the Irenaean picture predominates, as we see in the short summary passage in *A Science of God?*, at the end of the chapter on 'The God of Nature', although, characteristically, the supposition of necessity is qualified by a return to diffident agnosticism. Here is the passage in full:

> If I am challenged to say in one sentence why there are what men call natural disasters, I shall say this: it is because God makes the world make itself; or rather, since the world is not a single being, he makes the multitude of created forces make the world, in the process of making or being themselves. It is this principle of divine action that gives the world such endless vitality, such vital variety in every part. The price of it is, that the agents God employs in the basic levels of the structure will do what they will do, whether human convenience is

served by it or not. Yet the creative persuasion has brought it about that there is a world, not a chaos, and that in this world there are men. Would it have been possible for God to have made a world without a free-for-all of elemental forces at the bottom of it? I suppose not, but I do not know; and there is (I take it) only one Mind that does.[35]

John Hick, in the first edition of his big book on the problem of evil, *Evil and the God of Love*, has a short section on Farrer's *Love Almighty and Ills Unlimited*, in which he praises it as 'one of the best recent books on the problem of evil – perhaps the best'.[36] But he characterizes Farrer's theodicy as representing 'a basically Augustinian approach'. He cites Farrer's two parables and indeed stresses the Irenaean character of the second, which, of course, chimes in with Hick's own Irenaean approach; but he then alleges that Farrer repudiates both parables equally in favour of a reverent agnosticism. This does scant justice to Farrer's clear preference for the Irenaean parable, notwith-standing his repeated diffidence about pressing such why ques-tions, and it is a great pity that, in the second edition of *Evil and the God of Love*, Hick simply omitted the section on Farrer.

Let us stay, then, with the Irenaean parable and consider the idea that rooting and grounding God's personal creatures in a physical, evolving, universe and letting the human world make itself precisely in and through the processes of evolution and history are necessary conditions of the formation of any finite persons, with their own God-given being and nature, before ever they can be drawn into relation with their Maker and eventually immortalized. This idea constitutes an extension of the earlier suggestion that the values of specifically human life are inextricably bound up with the whole history of the uni-verse that both makes them possible and also forms the back-ground and conditions of particular life stories. It is now being suggested that some such process of formation is internal to the very being and nature of any finite personal life over against the creator – internal, at any rate, as far as the establishment and formation of finite persons are concerned. (I say 'some such process of formation', since it is unlikely that the actual evolv-ing universe is the only one capable of coming up with the conditions of life and personhood.) If it were indeed the case that creaturely persons could only be formed in some such way, then this would provide us with a very powerful theodicy indeed. For natural evil as well as moral evil could then be seen as inevitable by-products of any system necessary, not just for *our* formation, but for the formation of creaturely persons as such.

I now turn to the subject of divine providence, one of the main themes in Farrer's later writings, and I want to concentrate on what Farrer says in *A Science of God?* about God's providence in bringing cosmic and biological evolution to a climax in the formation of persons. This illustrates Farrer's understanding of double agency, the topic explored in depth by Edward Henderson in the last chapter. As Henderson explained, what Farrer means by double agency is the way in which divine creative and providential agency works in and through the energies and agencies of creatures. Double agency is certainly not confined, on Farrer's view, to the sphere of 'God's interaction with agents and not with the whole of creation', as John Polkinghorne asserts.[37] Certainly the grace–free will relation is the paradigm of double agency for Farrer; but it is the paradigm case of a relation which obtains at every level and at every phase of the creative process, not least in respect of evolution, as Farrer's treatment of that topic in *A Science of God?* and in the chapter on 'Providence and Evil' in *Saving Belief* makes clear. In no way does Farrer disparage evolutionary theory. Evolution is, for him, a supremely reasonable supposition. Gradual emergence is far more plausible than miraculous insertion. Evolution – cosmic and biological – is God's way of making the creature make itself, for very good reasons, as we have seen. But it does not follow that evolutionary theory can tell the whole story, when you consider the highest forms of life – Farrer mentions Shakespeare in this connection – that have developed from elementary systems of physical energy. When you consider all this, he observes, 'the case for a creative pull of some kind, drawing nature upwards, is a case that cannot be lightly dismissed'.[38] We cannot just assume that the evolution of higher forms is nothing but a natural process working itself out. What does it mean to say

that the mind of Shakespeare is implicitly contained in the interactions of inanimate substance? Clearly the fundamental energies of the universe have it in them to evolve the highest forms –
but by themselves and inevitably? Much more plausible is it to
suppose a hidden guidance or persuasion that makes creatures
make themselves and more. Farrer uses the language of persuasion in his summary treatment of this issue in *Saving Belief*. I
have already quoted his observation that 'Science studies the
pattern, but theology assigns the cause'. But this is how he goes
on to gloss that phrase 'the cause': 'that imperceptible persuasion exercised by creative Will on the chaos of natural forces,
setting a bias on the positive and achieving the creatures'.[39]
And, returning to *A Science of God?*, we find Farrer claiming
that God 'thinks all processes at every level into being themselves and into being themselves true to type. And yet without
faking the story or defying probability at any point he pulls the
history together into the patterns we observe.' The result, looking back from which we discern the hidden hand of God,
includes, of course, not only the evolution of life and the moral
and personal transcendence of which I spoke at the beginning
of this chapter, not only the creative heights typified by
Shakespeare, but also salvation history and the Incarnation.

Here are two more summary quotations from *A Science of
God?*: 'How are we to swallow the world's achievements of
pattern, as results due to no influence and proceeding from
no cause?' In fact, 'the pattern is scattered piecemeal over
the forces and events which make up the world; it is drawn
together and enjoyed as one in the mind of God'.[40]

This positing of hidden divine guidance or persuasion
extending in and through the whole story of cosmic and biological evolution, as well as of human history and the life stories
of individual agents, has a bearing on the question whether
intelligent life on Earth is unique. As I have written elsewhere,

In itself the notion of extraterrestrial intelligent life is perfectly coherent. The basic stuff and energies of the universe
unquestionably have it in them to combine and develop . . . in
such a way as to form the conditions for such life and to produce such life, as they manifestly have done on this planet.

And the vast number of galaxies similar to ours makes it highly likely that these conditions have been realized elsewhere and that other forms of intelligent life have evolved. This argument, however, is a purely statistical, probabilistic, argument, which presupposes that all the factors relevant to the evolution of intelligent life are known and are evenly distributed across the cosmos. But it may be the case that, while the stuff of the universe certainly has it in it to evolve intelligent life, it is highly unlikely actually to do so without some providential direction. The many extraordinary coincidences, from those factors in the early stages of cosmic evolution that have given rise to talk of an anthropic principle, through the many factors that have to coincide for there to be a stable, life-supporting environment, to the many factors that have to coincide if the higher organisms are to appear, may only be accountable for in terms of divine providence, and may well have only been realized once . . .[41]

These reflections, Farrer's and my own, also have a bearing on the ugly clash between evolutionary theory and creationism, especially in American schools. Clearly, Farrer would have no truck with doctrinaire rejection of evolutionary theory. Quite apart from the evidence in its favour, expounded persuasively by such writers as Richard Dawkins, evolutionary theory plays a crucial role in Farrer's own theodicy, as we have seen. But Farrer's work shows how acceptance of evolutionary theory in no way rules out a teleological view of nature. This can be seen at two stages in the picture Farrer builds up. In the first place, while evolutionary theory traces – maybe with some gaps still – the mechanisms and the processes whereby new life forms appear and develop, given the fundamental properties, powers and propensities of nature, and given the laws under which the basic energies operate, it has no explanation whatsoever for those properties, powers, propensities and laws being what they are. And in the second place, it fails to account for the highest forms of mind, personhood, morality and creativity, that is, for the ways in which the natural world eventually comes to transcend its natural origin and basis. As many writers and thinkers have shown, there is no insuperable contradiction between the theory of evolution and the doctrine of creation. Indeed the latter makes most sense of the former.

To conclude this chapter I want to ask to what extent Farrer, like many modern theologians, is to be understood as rejecting mind–body or soul–body dualism in his presentation of a theological anthropology. I will briefly compare Farrer's work, in this connection, with that of John Habgood in his book, *Being a Person*, subtitled *Where Faith and Science Meet*,[42] and that of David Braine, in his book, *The Human Person*, subtitled *Animal and Spirit*.[43]

John Habgood, a scientist turned theologian (and archbishop), presents us, in his Riddell Lectures, aimed at a general readership, with a clear and categorical rejection of mind–body or soul–body dualism, based on his understanding and acceptance of evolutionary theory, while at the same time showing how human animals have come to transcend their physical and biological origin in developing not only sense and consciousness but – through the acquisition of language – reason, choice, and spirituality as well. In rejecting not only dualism but also any form of reductionism where these higher capacities are concerned, Habgood insists that these mental, rational, and spiritual states and powers are states and powers, not of some incorporeal soul inserted in, or associated with, a highly developed animal organism, but of the human animal as such. As such, we are persons, made in God's image. And we find in Habgood, as in Farrer, much agonized wrestling with the problem of when this personhood is actually achieved or lost. Up to a point, I think Farrer would have agreed with Habgood's presentation. Another point of agreement would have been over the importance of interpersonal relationships in forming and sustaining our identity as persons. But I doubt if Farrer would have been happy with Habgood's suggestion that we can dispense altogether with talk of the human soul, replacing it with talk of our being what we are in the mind of God, that is to say, our identity being what it is precisely through the all-encompassing relationship to the whole of our lives in which God, our maker and redeemer, stands.[44]

What I think Farrer would have found missing in Habgood's account of being a person is reflection on human subjectivity, not least in its non-bodily aspects. For the states and powers of the human person, whereby we transcend our physical and biological origin, cannot simply be ascribed to the animal organism that we are, or, if they can, that entails a much more holistic conception of human beings as mental, as well as psychophysical, subjects of thought and action.

Such a holistic view is developed by the philosopher, David Braine, in his magisterial volume, *The Human Person*. Braine, like Habgood, is resolutely opposed to both materialism and dualism. But, unlike Habgood, he attempts to do full justice to the way in which each of us is the focalized subject of both psychophysical and non-bodily operations. Like other animals, we are subjects of sensation and emotion, psychophysical states and operations inextricably bound up with bodily existence. But, unlike other animals, human beings, through the development of language – here Braine is at one with both Habgood and Farrer – are subjects of non-bodily operations such as reasoning, will, and wonder. For much of his book, Braine explores the possibility of retaining the language of soul, not in terms of a separate substance but rather in terms of the incarnate subject of just those psychophysical and non-bodily operations that he has emphasized. To this end, he attempts to hold together an Aristotelian conception of the soul as the form of the body and a phenomenological conception of the soul as 'quasi-subsistent' subject. In the end, however, he prefers the language of person to that of soul, in so far as it captures the holistic nature of human existence, without denying the human subject's non-bodily operations which gave rise to the language of soul. To quote Braine, 'When a human being comes to be, we have the coming to be of a focalised subject of a nature to have operations which are not bodily, and thus the coming to be of a being whose *esse* transcends the body.'[45]

I think Farrer would have been sympathetic to Braine's account of the human person. But I think he would have wished to retain the language of soul. In *Finite and Infinite* he too used the Aristotelian language of the soul as the form of the body – itself a holistic concept of each kind of living creature's vital functions. 'The operation of the body', he wrote, 'is the immediate operation of the soul, or self.'[46] Again, in the same work,

Farrer insisted that the self is not a structure or a pattern but that which has these.[47] In an essay on 'Poetic Truth', reprinted in *Reflective Faith* and dating from the same period as *Finite and Infinite*, he wrote indifferently of soul, mind, and self. Of the soul, he wrote there: 'there is nothing of which we are more aware, for it is we ourselves'.[48] Interestingly, in *The Freedom of the Will*, he claimed that, even when we allow that consciousness is in large measure bound up with the physical, 'dualism breaks out in a new place'.

> You may seem to reduce the gap between 'body' and 'mind' by interpreting the workings of 'mind' in a bodylike manner. But only at a price – you open a hiatus in your thought about the mind itself. There is an area which the paraphysical story cannot be stretched to cover: that intimate province of the person which each of us is . . . The paraphysical account proves to be at best a diagram we make of mind-at-a-distance; it can never close in upon its object, or coalesce with the mind's own way of thinking itself.[49]

And in a late piece on 'Analogy in Common Talk', reprinted in *Interpretation and Belief*, Farrer insisted that in no way can I 'forgo the use of the pronoun "I" as common subject of my experience and acts'.[50] All the same, as Nancey Murphy has shown in Chapter 2, Farrer does not defend Cartesian dualism – the view of the soul as a separate substance. He shares, with both Habgood and Braine, a holistic view of the human person as a product, under God's providence, of evolution, even if, like Braine and unlike Habgood, he tries to do full justice to human subjectivity as 'the seat of consciousness'.

Farrer's retention of the language of soul leads me finally to ponder the nature of finite substance. After all, in *Finite and Infinite*, Farrer treated the will and the self as key features of finite substance.[51] And in later writings, right up to *Faith and Speculation*, these features of finite substance were to provide the prime analogies for his theology of God. Farrer would agree with Braine that the soul or self is not a separate substance. Rather, body and soul are, at present, different aspects of finite substance. But that must mean that the soul is more than 'quasi-subsistent'.[52] To cite Braine himself, the evolved human person is 'both animal and spirit'.[53] And it is *qua* spirit, as Habgood, Braine, and Farrer would allow, nay insist, that a human being is open to the gift of resurrection.

Notes

1 Lynne Truss, *Eats, Shoots & Leaves: The Zero Tolerance Approach to Punctuation*, London: Profile Books 2003.
2 Thomas F. Torrance, *Theological Science*, London: Oxford University Press 1969.
3 Austin Farrer, *Interpretation and Belief* (ed. Charles C. Conti), London: SPCK 1976, p. 3.
4 Austin Farrer, *The Glass of Vision*, London: Dacre Press 1948, p. 65.
5 Austin Farrer, *A Science of God?*, London: Geoffrey Bles 1966, p. 21.
6 Austin Farrer, *Love Almighty and Ills Unlimited*, London: Collins 1962, pp. 97f.
7 *A Science of God?*, p. 29.
8 *The Glass of Vision*, p. 66.
9 Austin Farrer, *Finite and Infinite*, London: Dacre Press 1943, p. 87.
10 Austin Farrer, 'Freedom and Theology', in *Reflective Faith*, London: SPCK 1972, pp. 163–70.
11 Austin Farrer, *The Freedom of the Will*, London: A. & C. Black 1958, p. 138.
12 Austin Farrer, *Reflective Faith*, p. 108.
13 *The Freedom of the Will*, p. 92.
14 Ibid., ch. III.
15 Austin Farrer, *Saving Belief*, London: Hodder & Stoughton 1964, p. 51.
16 Ibid., p. 70.
17 Ibid., p. 54.
18 Saul Kripke, *Naming and Necessity*. Oxford: Blackwell 1980. I am grateful to Douglas Hedley for reminding me of Kripke's argument.
19 Bertrand Russell, *The Analysis of Mind*, London: George Allen & Unwin 1921, p. 159.
20 *Love Almighty and Ills Unlimited*, pp. 106f.
21 *A Science of God?*, p. 101.
22 Ibid., p. 123.
23 *Love Almighty and Ills Unlimited*, p. 164.
24 Ibid., pp. 189–91.
25 Ibid., p. 190.

26 Ibid., p. 190.
27 See, e.g., Peter Singer, *Practical Ethics*, Cambridge: Cambridge University Press, 2nd edn 1993, ch. 2.
28 *Love Almighty and Ills Unlimited*, p. 189.
29 *Saving Belief*, p. 58.
30 Ibid., p. 52.
31 *Love Almighty and Ills Unlimited*, ch. IV.
32 Ibid., p. 66.
33 Ibid., p. 68.
34 Ibid., pp. 68–73.
35 *A Science of God?*, pp. 90f.
36 John Hick, *Evil and the God of Love*, London: Macmillan 1966, pp. 273–6.
37 John Polkinghorne, *Science and Providence*, London: SPCK 1989, p. 12.
38 *A Science of God?*, p. 45.
39 *Saving Belief*, p. 51.
40 *A Science of God?*, p. 81.
41 Brian Hebblethwaite, 'The Impossibility of Multiple Incarnations', *Theology* civ (2001), p. 331.
42 John Habgood, *Being a Person: Where Faith and Science Meet*, London: Hodder & Stoughton 1998.
43 David Braine, *The Human Person: Animal and Spirit*, London: Duckworth 1993.
44 Habgood, *Being a Person*, p. 224.
45 Braine, *The Human Person*, p. 540.
46 *Finite and Infinite*, p. 261.
47 Ibid., p. 261.
48 Austin Farrer, 'Poetic Truth', in *Reflective Faith*, p. 34.
49 *The Freedom of the Will*, p. 174.
50 Austin Farrer, 'Analogy in Common Talk', in *Interpretation and Belief*, p. 208.
51 *Finite and Infinite*, Part II.
52 Braine, *The Human Person*, p. 490.
53 See the subtitle of Braine's book and his treatment of the topic throughout.

5. The Role of Images in Theological Reflection

DAVID BROWN

This chapter is in three sections. The first considers why a religion like Christianity that is theoretically a religion of the word might none the less be right to give a more central place to images. The second then considers the question of how and why their content changes over the course of time, and possible criteria that might be employed for speaking of such change as legitimate or otherwise. Then finally in the last part of the chapter I look at the role of images in the context of what used to be called natural religion, human experience of the divine outside the context of the specifics of any particular revelation. Here my special focus will be on the extent to which conventional patterns of discussion in modern analytic philosophy of religion fail to reflect the range of that experience, and so are in as questionable a position about criteria as any purely theological discussion. Farrer has something to say on each of the three issues and what he says is important and valuable. Rather than simply endorsing his viewpoint, however, what I shall seek to do is develop his position, partly in response to my own recent writing.

The role of images

Farrer is keen to give a decisive role to images in both natural and revealed theology. The reasons that motivate him are clear. The modern alternatives lead to a wooden approach that is in the end destructive of religious belief. In the case of philosophy of religion conventional approaches are most likely to lead to God being treated like the infamous rabbit that is produced out of the conjurer's hat. In revealed theology propositional analyses, whether liberal or conservative, alike generate an atomistic approach that undermines the lively engagement with the text that is the appropriate response of religious belief. These two claims I want to return to in more detail in the next two sections. First, however, I want to try to clarify a little what Farrer puts in their place.

Given the long history of Christianity's critique of images and their association with idolatry, the reader unfamiliar with Farrer's thought might have expected a robust defence of the kind of image (painting and sculpture) under assault in the first iconoclastic controversy (in the eighth to ninth centuries) and again at the Reformation. This is not the case. Instead, despite his Anglo-Catholicism, Farrer continues to remain here close to his Baptist roots, for the images he has in mind are essentially verbal rather than visual.[1] We know that he had no interest in music,[2] and little interest in the visual arts.[3] By contrast, poetry fascinated him,[4] and it is clearly from this source that his talk of images is drawn. So we might paraphrase image in terms of metaphor, simile and analogy. Everything then depends on the verbal and what he can make of it.

Two features in particular seem to have attracted him: first, what might be termed the holistic, integrative character of images and, second, their openness to change. Farrer initially canvassed his ideas when Form Criticism was at the height of its popularity. The Form Critic dissects the text into small, discrete pericopes. Farrer by contrast sought a reintegration. Focusing on recurring images, he thought, offered a powerful strategy for asserting features that ran right through the text as whole and so could bond it together once more.[5] Again, their open-ended character allowed him to make some sense of changing approaches within the biblical text across time. There was continuity in the images but their application admitted of more than one interpretation in a way that more straightforward prose does not.

His general strategy must face some obvious criticisms. At the time the most common complaint was that his methodology resulted in the abandonment of the historical claims of Christianity: everything became mere metaphor. That was certainly very far from his intention. Indeed, his desire to uphold something like orthodox Christianity can scarcely be called into question. If he rightly protested that some images, such as that of the Trinity, cannot without loss be reduced to the purely literal, he was on less sure ground in trying to apply his methodology to the Bible as a whole; history and moral teaching, for instance, have their own distinctive claims.[6] Yet, from a contemporary perspective a more likely criticism is that he simply did not go far enough. Advocates of narrative theology might well suggest that the role of images is subordinate to the stories in which they are set and that therefore what really matters is the stories rather than the images that help to give them shape.[7] Indeed, the protest might be carried further into the claim that Farrer in focusing on image alone has already conceded too much to the dissectionist biblical scholar. However much images may link different stories, they remain small, discrete elements within a particular story and so encourage an atomistic approach.

Yet there are strengths in Farrer's position that narrative theology tends to lack. When the particular story is taken as a whole, it is very easy to fall into the trap of absolutizing its specific form in a manner no less trenchant than happens in more conservative advocacy of propositional revelation. Acceptance of the story at face value is seen as required, and no space therefore given for either critique or development in new directions.[8] Yet development is precisely what happens both in the history of the canon and in the Church's later history. That is why I personally prefer an expansion of Farrer's notion of image rather than narrative theology's move in what seems to me in the end a quite different direction. The more interesting question, for example, is not how Matthew's story of the wise men functions in its own right or how it fits into his narrative of the life of Jesus as a whole (important questions though these are), but rather the often radically different sorts of appropriation of the image made in the life of believers across the centuries. Their transformation into kings then becomes part of the open-ended character of the image, the continuity lying in the inclusion of the other or alien, now pursued in a new way.[9]

That particular example and its various permutations could be traced through Farrer's own chosen medium of poetry,[10] and indeed in many other verbal forms such as sermon illustrations. Equally, however, its open development could be pursued through the history of painting. It is at this point that Christianity's traditional objection to images might well be deployed: so far from opening options, the visual typically fore-closes them, enticing us to give absolute value to the merely pro-visional that is before us rather than encouraging us to look beyond and elsewhere. That this has sometimes happened in the history of art can scarcely be denied. But to concede this much is far from admitting that this is either commonly part of the artist's intention or indeed anything at all to do with the way visual art normally functions. Those unfamiliar with the medium tend to treat a canvas or sculpture as though it were at best intended as illustrative and at worse as a substitute for the reality itself. The truth could scarcely be more different. Almost all works of art in the history of Christianity have sought to engage the viewer and have done so precisely by leaving certain features open with encouragement to further exploration.[11] Numerous examples could be given without difficulty, and there is thus in my view a precise parallel with Farrer's own pre-ferred literary image. Indeed, it is salutary to recall the way in which some Hindu theologians want to recall their own faith community to the visual precisely on the grounds that com-pared with the restrictions imposed by language it is its visual images that are inherently the more open.[12]

It is no part of my intention here to overthrow Christianity's conventional understanding of itself as a religion of the word, but it does seem to me that Farrer, in stressing the importance of images, has identified an important issue, the need to redress the balance. We think through our imaginations no less than we do by more logical, analytical ways of thinking, and extending that insight to visual as well as verbal imagery could only strengthen Farrer's point. I have already acknowledged that by no means every aspect of the Bible and its claims can be treated in this way. None the less, it is worth emphasizing how much can be. It is not just Farrer's own preferred types such as king, son of man, shepherd and lamb, but also, particularly if my proposed visual expansion is accepted, most of the major incidents in Scripture, as also much of Jesus' teaching, couched as it was in the form of stories.

If the question is turned round, and reasons sought for why God might prefer this method of communication with humanity rather than any other, it is surely not hard to detect possible answers. Part of the explanation must lie, as Farrer himself notes, in the limitations of language, that the purely literal inevitably fails to capture as radically different a being as God. If that is an answer that has often been given over the centuries, a more modern response is also possible, the need to explain changes in understanding both within the biblical canon and beyond. Previous generations had no difficulty in finding numerous anticipations of the New Testament in the Old, and that pattern was repeated in the history of the Church as the novel was given the character of the old and long-established.[13] Modern historical consciousness prevents us from taking that line. Images, however, can help us see how such change might have taken place, and indeed be given divine endorsement. If I may put it like this, images allow the coaxing of the individual beyond where present understanding has reached in a way that is less possible with a fixed meaning, where believers are likely to see themselves in a situation not of engagement but rather of confrontation and conflict with established authority, and so are more likely to back off than explore further.[14] In other words, the openness of the image permits some sense of the new already being there, and so makes change less traumatic and easier to bear. It is to this phenomenon of change and Farrer's response to it that I now turn.

The capacity of images for change

Farrer seems to envisage a starting point for revelation in universal archetypes that are then progressively modified until they take their decisive form in the life of Christ and in apostolic reflection on that life.[15] So, for example, sacred kingship is a well-nigh universal way of treating authority figures in early societies. To begin with, reflection on that particular image of kingship is mediated for the Israelites through their own kings, especially David. The loss of the monarchy, however, leads to a new understanding in the eagerly awaited, anointed Messiah, which in turn is then further modified by Christ's conception of his own inauguration of the kingdom of God. In trying to comprehend such developments, Farrer is insistent on an indispensable divine contribution, particularly through divine inspiration in the events surrounding Jesus' life and their immediate aftermath. However, Farrer has little to say on the divine role as such.[16] Instead, his focus is on the psychological processes involved. Just as wit is given shape by reason in the natural sphere, so in the supernatural it seems to be a case of imagination been shaped by memory. In new contexts certain familiar images come to mind once more. Interacting with the new context a new version and content is the result.

By memory is intended not just earlier uses of the image most pertinent to the context in question but other images that may also contribute to its modification.[17] Indeed, in terms of criteria for legitimacy of talk of revelation, Farrer is clear that compatibility with other endorsed images is one possible test of the appropriateness of a new development, as is also compatibility with the type of God given by natural reason.[18] The latter we shall come to in due course. Here suffice it to note that his heavy reliance on earlier uses of the same or related imagery has led some scholars to talk of Farrer's approach as really one of intertextuality. Indeed, some have claimed to detect an anticipation of structuralist forms of exegesis.[19] While this leads one scholar of English literature – Frank Kermode – to a warm appreciation of what he believes Farrer was attempting, another – Dame Helen Gardner – took a much more negative view.[20]

In their interchange it is possible to read Gardner's comments as amounting to no more than a conservative's desire for more stress on historicity, but rather more was, I think, at stake. In any case, as already noted, Farrer did not deny the importance of history to Christianity. He seems, for instance to have accepted a physical account of the resurrection.[21] Also, while insisting on the symbolic significance of Jesus' miracles, he refused to countenance Bultmann's ruling out *tout court* the possibility that violations of laws of nature might also be involved.[22] The more interesting disagreement between them in my view lies not on the question of historicity as such but rather over the extent to which these new contexts might continue to allow to the images a genuine openness. Gardner is insistent upon the uniqueness of reflection in any specific context, and refuses to countenance generation simply out of what has gone before, whereas Farrer's methodology constantly seeks for precedents in the past.[23] Indeed, his suggestions for reading Mark's Gospel and the Book of Revelation (his two most extended studies), presuppose in author and reader alike an astonishingly detailed knowledge of earlier scriptural texts. So, for example, the last two Greek words of Mark's original ending (*ephobounto gar*) are meant immediately to call to mind Joseph's brothers' first reaction on meeting up once more with their brother in Egypt, or again careful counting of the number of miracles in Mark is supposed to alert the reader to an allusion to the resurrection.[24] Farrer himself became dissatisfied with some of his earlier attempts at numerology.[25] In any case, the lack of parallels in literature of the time make one question whether either the authors or readers could ever have quite thought like this. This is not to dismiss Farrer's exegesis in general. He argues well for the view that Mark so effectively anticipates the resurrection in the rest of his Gospel that there was no need for any ending other than the mysterious 16.8. Again, the use of symbolist motifs throughout all four Gospels is now much more widely accepted. The problem rather is Farrer's attempt to make the Scriptures entirely self-contained. There is, for example, little reference in Farrer to a common theme in contemporary biblical scholarship of the New Testament's debt to intertestamental Judaism.

That narrower focus has been noted by others. Although in response to the question of papal infallibility, Farrer speaks favourably of post-biblical developments into a greater truth, it is not an issue to which he devotes any sustained attention in his writings.[26] Some have sought to extend his theory of inspiration into the work of successive generations of readers, either at an individual level or more corporately in the life of the Church, but in neither case has this been done in a way that also tries to develop his notion of open-ended images.[27] That seems to me essential for a number of reasons. The first is the sheer fact of continuing change. I have already mentioned one small example, the way in which the wise men were transformed into kings, but far more substantial instances are not wanting. There is, for instance, now much wider acknowledgement than there was in Farrer's day of the extent to which the doctrine of the Trinity is a postbiblical development.[28] But coupled with such facts is the increasing implausibility of the way in which the Church currently argues for new readings of its scriptural deposit. The equality of the sexes, for example, is after all really there, it is said, despite the failure of any of the Church's major theologians to recognize this over two thousand years of the Church's history.[29] Again, the claim is made that the doctrine of hell as a place of eternal punishment was not after all part of the original meaning of Christ's teaching.[30] Similarly, Christ's identification with us in our suffering is treated as a fundamental aspect of the gospel's proclamation when there is only a couple of verses in the whole canon that could even conceivably be interpreted in this way, and so on.[31]

What is surely needed is some account that takes seriously the obvious meaning of the texts, and yet argues for the legitimacy of going beyond them. However inadequately, that is what I have attempted to provide in two recent volumes, where, although Farrer is not mentioned, I have taken seriously his stress on the power of images and their capacity to generate new meanings. Where I differ is first in insisting that the process did not stop with the closure of the canon, and second in stressing the key role of factors extraneous to the texts themselves. If a little bit of jargon may be forgiven, I suggest that we call those factors triggers. Farrer, of course, did acknowledge some, such as the fall of the monarchy, but these remain essentially internal to the story of revelation, whereas what I think needs to be conceded is what a key role quite extraneous factors play, whose impact then needs to be incorporated into the Christian story.

Some examples should help. Take something as central as the way in which Christ is perceived, and in particular his childhood and crucifixion. Despite our deeply embedded assumptions that the New Testament shows a profound interest in Christ's childhood, most New Testament scholars would readily concede that the motive for Matthew and Luke's infancy narratives lies essentially elsewhere, as prologues to his adult life.[32] Certainly, that would seem confirmed by the earlier history of Christian art in which Jesus is consistently portrayed simply as a mini-adult. Contrast the second millennium, and all the intimacy and tenderness of childhood is now there.[33] Again, so far as the crucifixion is concerned, as a rough generalization one may say that for the first thousand years of Christianity it was Jesus' representative role that interested the artist, one in which he is depicted as the unassailable conqueror of sin and death, whereas in the second millennium increasingly it is his identification with us in our suffering that is evoked, most obviously perhaps in the culmination of this trend with Grünewald's Isenheim Altarpiece at the beginning of the sixteenth century.[34] In explaining why such changes occurred, it just will not do to appeal to the impact of the Scriptures by themselves. Matthew's and Luke's narratives were in part triggered to be read differently by the different way in which children were now being perceived as valuable in their own right. That was a slow process which matured across the centuries, to which there were many contributing causes. But it was scarcely in any case the only factor. Like changes in presentation of the crucifixion there was the desire for a more personal or individualistic religion which reflected wider changes in society. The revival of town life and greater social mobility meant that individuals thought of themselves less as part of larger units and more in their own highly particular identity. A Christus Victor therefore now seemed less pertinent than a Saviour with whom one could interact in affective piety. So despite the absence of any New Testament references to such an identification as a reason for the Incarnation, the Bible was in fact now read in this way, as claiming that God had become incarnate to identify with us in our suffering.

Acknowledging triggers of such a kind, however, makes all the more pressing the question of why it was appropriate that their effects should be absorbed within the Christian tradition. Farrer, in keeping the story a purely internal one, at least successfully by-passed that question, if on inadequate grounds. It is here that another piece of jargon becomes useful, that of trajectories, aspects within the Scriptures that might point in that direction even if they do not in themselves speak of or imply any such move. In this case it may be observed that it is a basic claim of the New Testament that Christ has salvific consequences for every aspect of life. So it would seem not unnatural to apply such a principle to new areas such as these (childhood and suffering) once they come to be seen in a certain kind of way. Of course the argument has its limitations. It is the same sort of consideration that has led some to argue that Jesus must be portrayed with feminine attributes as in female Christas or as having homosexual inclinations if certain concerns are to be addressed. That is why any such argument needs to be augmented by other trajectories, such as the danger of adoptionism unless the Incarnation is treated as having full significance for the whole of Jesus' earthly life.

Not that the criteria need always be christological. Take the decline of belief in hell as a place of eternal punishment or the rise in belief in equality of the sexes. In the former case relevant triggers would include the replacement of natural law by the new focus on natural rights as also the later growth in notions of limited liability.[35] Again, changes in attitudes to women have been triggered by the experience of women in positions of education and responsibility, all made possible by wider changes in society such as far more women working independently of men as a result of the Industrial Revolution. In the latter case I have argued that the trajectory that made the difference here was the New Testament principle of equality of regard being widened to include equality of status, once there was seen to be no relevant difference justifying different treatment for men and for women. Hell is a more difficult issue. For here it would seem more a case of new theories of punishment turning back upon the New Testament to offer a critique, and so requiring modification of a particular doctrine. For some that might seem an unacceptable implication to draw. Yet elsewhere no qualms have been felt about accepting the possibility that newly determined natural knowledge might necessitate modification of what is taken to be the import of the meaning of Scripture. An obvious case in point is the way in which scientific discoveries have forced on us new readings of the opening chapters of Genesis.

Clearly not all of these developments have images in either the literary or the visual sense as their primary focus. So my claim is certainly not that images are always the primary revelatory medium through which God should be seen to operate. None the less this appears true much more widely than is commonly currently conceded. Take the move in Christianity, Islam and Judaism alike to change the primary focus of the story of Abraham's sacrifice of Isaac from the father to the son. If the internal route is followed, one might say that for Christianity the pressure came from the desire to present Isaac as an anticipatory type for Christ. But this won't do, as the change antedates Christianity; and there is little doubt in my mind that it is the visual horror of imagining a young child being offered that led to the substitution in all three religions of a young or even mature adult who could make his own decision in an act of self-sacrifice.[36] That is a change that is already occurring during the time of the formation of the biblical canon. The decline in customary understandings of hell comes very much later.

Irrespective of whether such changes are accepted as legitimate or not, they do both raise acutely the issue of distorting images. The following dilemma seems to present itself: either the imagination misled in the past, or else it does so at the later stage as alternative understandings assume prominence. However, a 'both . . . and' answer is surely a possibility. It is not so much that Abraham's willingness to offer what he holds most dear is rejected; rather, it is seen as less perfect than the offering of oneself, the *raison d'être* behind the later model. Again, as I have argued elsewhere at length, images of hell in the Church's tradition brought not just pessimism and damnation but also strategies of interdependence in warding off the threat, as well as a far stronger sense of the need for self-judgement than is to be found anywhere in the New Testament.[37] Despite surface appearances, the persistence of the image did therefore contribute positively to producing a more humane religion.

One direction one might go at this point is to an examination of how an image approach might facilitate dialogue between the religions. Although the Isaac story is an easy example to take, it does illustrate the way in which exploration of the history and varying functions of an image might resolve apparent deep-seated conflict into a much closer affinity. However, Farrer eschewed such questions, and so instead I turn now to the role of images in natural religion, in giving us a general sense of the divine in the first place.

Natural religion and philosophy of religion's limitations

In his more philosophical works Farrer appears to move progressively away from conventional Thomism.[38] Even in his earliest he has abandoned any claim to proof, and instead identifies philosophy's role as clarifying reasons for belief. However, these reasons still follow closely the kind of formal considerations that Thomas offered, whereas in his later writings Farrer adopts what has been called his voluntarist position, with much stress on the divine will, and our experience of God located primarily in personal situations, and in particular by contrast with the limits of our will or in the stretching of its capacities in creativity.[39] My doubt here would once more be whether he went far enough, this time in his revolt against Thomism. It is almost as though he wished to produce an alternate inner core, with at times nature deliberately demoted in contrast to personal interchange, and then even personal interchange firmly subordinated to the internal evidence of prayer.[40] Again, in his anxiety to secure something like the Christian God, he consistently introduces terms such as 'infinite', 'personal' and so on, whereas human religious experience, I would suggest, is far more diverse and tentative. Acknowledging that fact, so far from weakening his claims for religious belief, would, I contend, actually strengthen them.

Philosophers like to believe their discipline immune to the type of cultural conditioning that plagues other areas of discussion, but there is little reason to think this so. It is not that validity of arguments is affected but rather which are chosen and so on. In a fascinating book the Cambridge philosopher Edward Craig has drawn attention to influence in what for many must seem a surprising direction, not philosophy affecting our concept of God but rather the Christian doctrine of the image of

God in human beings apparently having an impact on how purely secular issues in philosophy have been pursued.[41] More pertinent here, and gist to Farrer's mill, would be Michael Buckley's contention in his book *At the Origins of Modern Atheism* that the presentation of arguments for God's existence as foundational arguments is in fact only a relatively recent phenomenon in modern Western culture, and, as Farrer also claimed, based on false assumptions about how our thinking ought to operate.[42] God is not an inference from other experience, but an already existing experience in search of a deeper foundation.

That said, it is all the more surprising therefore that Farrer confines relevant images to almost the same narrow range as the analytic philosopher of religion. Other theologians have done likewise. For Schleiermacher, for instance, what might be called the cosmological experience was central to his theology. Others, however, have been more adventurous. Rahner appeals to a great range of what he calls transcendent experiences, while Tillich uses his principle of correlation to ground belief in God in metaphysical situations of conflict that could, he believes, only have their resolution in God, if at all.[43] Yet even with these two last examples the desire to establish something like the Christian God leads, it seems to me, to focus on a very much narrower range than what humanity has in fact in its history identified as experience of the divine.

I say this not to weaken such claims but rather to draw attention to the way in which theological discussion no less than philosophical actually distorts reality and thereby inadvertently weakens the case for religious belief. I am in any case unsure what exactly could be meant by an experience of absolute dependence or again of infinite personhood as distinct from a very much greater or larger being than ourselves, but let that pass. My worry is that by encouraging focus exclusively on something like those experiences, the great mass of religious experience is thereby demoted, and the exceptional elevated as necessary in order to found religious belief. It also encourages believers to misread their experience as though only the exceptional can count as contact with God rather than that being the normal pattern of everyday living.

Take ordinary experiences of immanence and transcendence. These may be mediated through nature or through human artefacts such as music or architecture. The latter are often treated as though they were necessarily less persuasive but of course the architecture may well have been construed precisely with this thought in mind, of evoking or paralleling the conditions in nature that might make such an experience a possibility. A Gothic church may give you a sense of otherness and of being pulled into an alternative reality, but it is unlikely of itself to suggest a personal reality or an infinite one for that matter, whereas vast, sublime landscapes of the type popularized in the paintings of Casper David Friedrich or the Boston River School may well raise questions of infinity but again not necessarily those of personhood.[44] Likewise, experiences of divine immanence can take numerous forms. To assume that they entail pantheism is to make the same kind of mistake as those who use transcendent experience to establish the Christian God. The immanent experience can of itself only suggest a small part of reality suffused with God. Baroque architecture mediates experiences of exuberance, variety and fecundity, none of which require personhood, while a luxuriant harvest crop may well evoked a sense of providential care and thereby lead naturally into notions of the personal.[45] Plotinus or impersonal forms of Hinduism cannot therefore simply be ruled out of court from the start.

I am introducing all this variety of experience here not to exclude a personal and infinite God, but rather as a way of underlining the fact that experiences that carry no such entailment are not therefore without significance. The experience could still have such a being as its source, even though in this case no such aspects have been disclosed. Perhaps the point can be made clearest by taking another common type of experience that seldom gets into the relevant sections of philosophical and theological discussions, that of thankfulness. In the days before the Research Assessment Exercise (RAE) and the numerous other government checks now required on academic conduct one happily put in extra hours for institutions, grateful for what was mediated through them, but the experience of the institution did not reveal any to whom gratitude was especially due for things being the way they were. Of course, that might argue for the inappropriateness of the attitude and therefore the inappropriateness of similar religious attitudes of gratitude for life as a gift and so on. But in fact in the case of institutions, though it is true that no particular individual could be identified, it is also the case that there were people who tried to keep things the way they were, just as others were responsible for introducing change. So there was the personal behind the experience, although the experience as such did not help in identifying any particular individual or individuals in such a role; similarly, then, in the religious case. Thankfulness for a graced life, whether viewed personally or not, is in fact a common motivation for religious belief and action; yet it seldom, if ever, obtains either appropriate recognition or analysis.

Again, think of responses connected with place. A number of Continental philosophers have connected feelings of being at home in a particular place and religion, and one can see why.[46] Of course, sometimes no more is meant than one is content with one's environment, or perhaps one setting within a particular society, but often something very much larger is at stake. The place evokes a sense of one's total context being right. One's situatedness is more than mere accident; the place reflects the pattern of a larger design to one's life. Again, that can complement or contrast with a feeling of the provisionality of one's setting, what is felt as a pressing summons to do other things, to be elsewhere, and that also has its religious outlet in the phenomenon of pilgrimage, which, intriguingly, despite the initial hostility of a number of major religions, was eventually to find a place in each one of them.[47]

I mention these less conventional cases not to decry experiences of cosmological dependence or natural design but to indicate how in focusing on a few standard cases the philosophical theologian actually distorts the shape of human experience. For most people throughout most of history God has not been the exceptional event, but very much the norm, and precisely because of the great range of forms through which the divine has been mediated. Even in modern Western society this may still be true to a much wider extent than religion's cultured despisers suppose, as the recent census figures may possibly indicate.[48] Certainly, nowadays there are serious cultural inhibitors. Weber himself suggested the decline of religion inevitable, as instrumental rationality becomes in modern society the universal standard against which all is measured.[49] With everything always seen as a means towards some further end quite different sorts of question, quite different images, are now to the fore: how, for example, a building might best serve the practicalities of the liturgy rather than how it might mediate God in its own right. The sadness is that such more immediate preoccupations may well prevent openness to the possibility of immanence or transcendence being mediated through the building within which the liturgy is set, however inspiring or august it may be.

Perhaps, however, it is not too late to view our world in the way it was once viewed, and in this Farrer indeed can give us a lead. It is just that he failed to carry his argument far enough. Take his own preferred case of the personal and love. Farrer wanted to push immediately towards infinite love. But limited human love might of itself mediate experience of the divine. Such at all events is the suggestion of two contemporary popular musicians who have both independently come up with the same idea. For Al Green and Nick Cave alike it is unnecessary to sing of God (though both occasionally do); their love songs are already for them just such an experience.[50]

All this may seem a long way from images, but it is not. Farrer revolted from the rather narrow range on offer from Aquinas in his Five Ways. Even so he advanced little beyond the personal and the analogical. God, however, can be seen operating much more widely.[51] Christopher Smart found God in his cat, Paul Cézanne – after his conversion – in a mountain (Mont Sainte Victoire), Pindar in the grace of an athlete's body, Frank Lloyd Wright in prairie houses, Nick Cave in a love song, and so on. Most of these are, significantly, visual images. Earlier I suggested that the image is in fact inherently more open-ended than the word, and so potentially less liable to idolatry, and that despite Christianity's historical claims to the contrary. The irony is that in both areas I have discussed (revelation and natural religion) this seems also true. It is the theologian who confines revelation to the verbal who is most likely to constrict

God's further action or else project back what is not really there. It is the verbally minded philosopher who insists on the least visual of images that in the end confines God to the margins of human experience. Farrer's writings contain those warnings. In our own day we now need to carry his insights further.

Notes

1 His father was a Baptist minister. Farrer pays him a warm tribute in *The End of Man*, London: SPCK 1973, p. 69.

2 For his lack of interest in music, see Stephen Platten, 'Diaphanous Thought: Spirituality and Theology in the Work of Austin Farrer' in *Anglican Theological Review* 69 (1987), p. 47, n. 84. Yet music does have the power to generate images, not only where it is specifically written with such an aim in view but also where others have made the association as, for example, in some of the ballets of Frederick Ashton.

3 Significantly, in a sermon on 'Epstein's Lazarus' his approach is indirect, through a poem about the statue, and even then he says virtually nothing about the sculpture as such: *The End of Man*, pp. 25–9.

4 Platten provides an extensive list of the poets Farrer quotes and knows: 'Diaphanous Thought', pp. 33–4.

5 Farrer speaks of the Form Critic turning Mark into 'a hack editor' who handed on to us 'an impersonal and disjointed mass of tradition': *A Celebration of Faith*, London: Hodder & Stoughton 1970, p. 41.

6 The problem here is that symbolic treatments can easily give the impression that writers are playing fast and loose with the 'facts' in order to produce appropriate equivalences.

7 The need to recover a unified narrative is one of the leading themes of Hans Frei's *The Eclipse of Biblical Narrative*, New Haven: Yale University Press 1974.

8 Not that this is an inevitable feature of narrative theology. Like Farrer, Brevard Childs' canonical criticism wrestled with change in the way stories are told, though even he wants to call closure at some point (differently nuanced in his successive writings). Contrast his more recent publications with *Introduction to the Old Testament as Scripture*, London: SCM Press 1979.

9 Whereas Matthew's magi with their astrology are used to represent pagan aspirations, the kings stand in for wealth and the foreigner (the three then known races).

10 As in Langston Hughes' 'Carol of the Brown King' the concluding verse of which makes the affective point quite directly: 'The Wise Men/ One dark like me/ Part of His/ Nativity.'

11 In the case of the wise men, for example, their transformation is not merely into kings but also into the three different ages (young, middle-aged, and old) that need to acknowledge their need of Christ. If such changes encourage engagement on the part of the viewer, so too do some more specific explorations, such as the kings being given the features of the Medici family by Bennozo Gozzoli in their own private chapel.

12 For an early precedent, see the writings of the ninth-century poet-saint, Manikkavacakar. For the contrast with Aquinas, R. H. Davies, *Lives of Indian Images*, Princeton: Princeton University Press 1997, pp. 32–3.

13 Examples of the latter phenomenon are given later in this essay. Perhaps the best example of the former is the use of the Old Testament at carol services, where the prophets are unlikely to have had any such notions in mind. For some more general reflections on this phenomenon, see my *The Word to Set You Free*, London: SPCK 1995, pp. 17–21.

14 Farrer talks of 'hidden means of appropriation' and of effects 'at a sub-conscious level': *A Rebirth of Images*, London: Dacre Press 1949, p. 13. The point is that, if we are not fully aware of what is going on, resistance may well be less likely.

15 The language of 'archetype' is quite common. For example, he describes 'the God of Moses' as 'the divine archetype of a tribal patri-arch': *Interpretation and Belief* (ed. Charles C. Conti), London: SPCK 1976, p. 41.

16 'In inspired wit a spark leaps from intelligence to intelligence across a field of imagination': *The Glass of Vision*, London: Dacre Press 1948, p. 25.

17 See *The Glass of Vision*, esp. pp. 134–6, 146. Context and subordi-nate images subtly change 'the master-images', for 'it is only through images already implanted that revelation grows'. (136).

18 *The Glass of Vision*, pp. 110–11: 'this idea of a supreme being as a canon to interpret revelation . . . the principal images provide a canon to the lesser images'.

19 E.g. 'it is the structuralist who looks back to Farrer': D. Jasper, *Coleridge as Poet and Religious Thinker*, London: Macmillan 1985, p. 149.

20 Described as a 'most elegant interpretation' in F. Kermode, *The Genesis of Secrecy*, Cambridge, Mass.: Harvard University Press 1979, pp. 60–4, esp. 60. Gardner criticizes Farrer in the second of her Riddell lectures in *The Limits of Literary Criticism*, London:

Oxford University Press 1956, and renews her critique in her *In Defence of the Imagination*, Oxford: Clarendon Press 1984.

21 'An English Appreciation' in H. W. Bartsch (ed.), *Kerygma and Myth*, New York: Harper & Row 1961, p. 220.

22 Ibid., p. 216.

23 Here I agree with the general thrust of H. Hauge's argument in his 'The Sin of Reading: Farrer, Gardner, Kermode' in A. Loades and M. McLain (eds), *Hermeneutics: The Bible and Literary Criticism*, London: Macmillan 1992, pp. 113–28.

24 For the conclusion of Mark taking up the Septuagint's account of Joseph and his brothers: *The Glass of Vision*, pp. 114–15. For the role of Markan miracles: *A Study in Mark*, London: Dacre Press 1951, esp. pp. 30–52, esp. 52. He finds 13 a recurring symbol of a new inclusiveness (the 12 tribes plus the Gentiles), and so suggests that with 12 healing miracles Mark intended the resurrection to be read as the greatest healing of them all.

25 *St Matthew and St Mark*, London: Dacre Press 1966, simplifies the approach of the earlier *Study*. Again his later commentary on *The Revelation of St John the Divine*, Oxford: Oxford University Press 1964, substantially modified the complexities of his earlier *A Rebirth of Images*.

26 'Infallibility and historical revelation' in *Interpretation and Belief*, pp. 151–64, esp. 163.

27 See the essays by Ingolf Dalferth and Gerard Loughlin in Loades and McLain, *Hermeneutics*, pp. 71–112.

28 I have sought to tackle this issue in *The Divine Trinity*, London: Duckworth 1985, and in a number of subsequent articles.

29 See my *Discipleship and Imagination*, Oxford: Oxford University Press 2000, pp. 11–31, esp. 12–19. I argue that both its immediate context and its wider setting in the thought of Paul make modern interpretations of Galatians 3.28 implausible.

30 Again, highly implausible in my view: see the same volume, pp. 130–6.

31 Hebrews 2.18 and 4.15. I argue elsewhere that they mean no such thing: *Tradition and Imagination*, Oxford: Oxford University Press 1999, pp. 360–2.

32 So, for example, Raymond Brown in his *Birth of the Messiah*, London: Geoffrey Chapman 1993 edn, esp. pp. 585–6, 620.

33 The contrast is pursued at length in *Tradition and Imagination*, pp. 75–105.

34 For this contrast, ibid., pp. 345–64.

35 For the way in which the acceptance of limited liability in English economic law had ramifications for the doctrine of hell, see B. Hilton, *The Age of Atonement*, Oxford: Clarendon Press 1988, pp. 255–97.

36 Discussed in *Tradition and Imagination*, pp. 237–60.

37 *Discipleship and Imagination*, pp. 130–71.

38 Jeffrey Eaton has helpfully analysed these developments in some detail in his *The Logic of Theism*, Lanham, MD: University Press of America 1980, pp. 1–72. In particular he contrasts Farrer's earlier position in *Finite and Infinite*, London: Dacre Press 1943, with that in *Faith and Speculation*, London: A. & C. Black 1967.

39 In *Faith and Speculation* Unconditioned Will replaces Necessary Being: God is he 'who is all he wills to be, and wills to be all he is' (118). This is partially anticipated in his *The Freedom of the Will*, London: A. & C. Black 1958. The divine image in human beings was a recurring theme in his sermons. For this stress on the personal, see further E. H. Henderson, 'Valuing in Knowing God: An Interpretation of Austin Farrer's Religious Epistemology', *Modern Theology* 3 (1985), pp. 165–82.

40 For nature demoted, cf. *A Celebration of Faith*, pp. 73–4. For life in God as 'self-authenticating', *Faith and Speculation*, p. 129. It is here that Charles Hefling's comparison with Bonaventure is most persuasive: *Jacob's Ladder*, Cambridge, Mass.: Cowley 1979, pp. 20–43, esp. 38–9.

41 Edward Craig, *The Mind of God and the Works of Man*, Oxford: Clarendon Press 1987.

42 Michael J. Buckley, *At the Origins of Modern Atheism*, New Haven: Yale University Press 1987.

43 For a brief comparison of their three approaches, see my *Continental Philosophy and Modern Theology*, Oxford: Blackwell 1987, pp. 1–6.

44 For extended discussion of transcendence and immanence mediated through architecture, see my *God and Enchantment of Place*, Oxford: Oxford University Press 2004, pp. 245–371. For Friedrich and the Boston River School, ibid., pp. 113–18.

45 As in the paintings and etchings of Samuel Palmer, e.g. 'Cornfield by Moonlight': Raymond Lister, *Samuel Palmer: His Life and Art*, Cambridge: Cambridge University Press 1987, p. 46.

46 Most notably, Heidegger, but also Bachelard, de Certeau, Foucault and Irigiray: for references, see *God and Enchantment of Place*, pp. 188–9.

47 For a discussion of God mediated through experiences of place and pilgrimage, ibid., pp. 153–244.

48 In the British census of 2000, 76 per cent of the population declared itself adherents of one faith or another, and 72 per cent Christian.

49 What Weber called *Zweckrationalität*, and which he connects with *Entzauberung* or the 'disenchantment' of the world. See further his essay 'Science as a vocation' in H. H. Gerth and C. Wright Mills

(eds), *From Max Weber*, London: Routledge & Kegan Paul 1948, pp. 129–56.

50 N. Cave, 'The Secret Life of the Love Song' in *The Complete Lyrics 1978–2001*, London: Penguin 2001, pp. 1–19. Note, for instance, his comment that all love songs 'address God, for it is the haunted premise of longing that the true Love Song inhabits' (7). For Al Green's somewhat different approach, D. Erhlich, *Inside the Music*, Boston: Shambhala 1997, pp. 172–9.

51 I attempt to purpose in more detail the questions raised by the third part of this paper in 'Experience Skewed' in K. Vanhoozer and M. Warner (eds), *Transcending Boundaries in Philosophy and Theology*, London: Ashgate 2005.

6. Austin Farrer's Shaping Spirit of Imagination

DOUGLAS HEDLEY

Tell me where is fancy bred,
Or in the heart or in the head?
How begot, how nourished?
Reply, Reply.

(Shakespeare, *Merchant of Venice* III ii 63)

It requires little justification to discuss the thought of arguably the greatest English theologian of the twentieth century, Austin Farrer. Yet Farrer is in many respects an enigmatic and elusive writer. He belonged to no clearly defined school of theology and did not found one. His elegant and sometimes epigrammatic prose does not flinch from real puzzles and apparent paradoxes. Farrer relentlessly fuses poetry, metaphysics and Scripture in his theology, brooding on images and ideas – often arguing in imaginary dialogues. A writer of great spiritual depth, his intellect is decisive and acute, fertile and suggestive. This chapter will consider Farrer from two perspectives. First, it explores the profundity of his thought in the light of the English Romantic inheritance. And second, it considers the fertility of Farrer's intellectual legacy through the prism of Basil Mitchell's philosophy of religion. I shall concentrate on Mitchell's *Faith and Criticism,* and suggest that his philosophy of religion is, in part, a creative instance of Farrer's rich legacy in philosophical theology.

Faith and Criticism

In *Faith and Criticism* Basil Mitchell observes that Schleier-macher's strategy of surrendering to science all concern with explanation and reserving to religion some quite distinct domain no longer has the obviousness which was once claimed for it.[1] Yet Karl Barth did just that. It is, perhaps, one of the ironies of the history of theology that Barth was continuing Schleiermacher's project of immunizing theology from critique. Equally peculiar is the fact that the influence of postmodern thought in theology has frequently reinforced the strategy of pleading for the idea of theology's immunity from rational criticism. Just as MacIntyre once combined Barth with logical positivism, so contemporary avant-garde philosophical theologians who want to defend orthodoxy tend to combine Barth with Derrida or Foucault, for just the same reasons. Philosophy, for many postmodern theologians, is then not so much the handmaiden as the Cinderella of faith.

Basil Mitchell in *Faith and Criticism* defends (to my mind) the vastly more compelling idea of the reciprocity of faith and criticism: 'Without faith in an established tradition criticism has nothing to fasten on; without criticism the tradition ceases in the end to have any purchase on reality' (88). Mitchell characteristically uses a naval image: Christian apologetics after the Enlightenment is akin to navigating a river. Shall the captain of the ship go to the right (rationalistic) bank or turn to the left (fideistic) position? He envisages four options: first, sailing past Hume and Kant fideistically. This position Mitchell, like Farrer, rejects. In fact he quotes Farrer's epigram, 'God cannot be trusted to exist' (65) to this effect. Second, reductionism – one can jettison much of the inherited cargo. This was the move of Don Cupitt. Third, one can reject the attempt to navigate the river. Fourth – and this is Mitchell's own position – one can survey the shoals and see whether the danger still exists. That is to say that one scrutinizes the challenge posed by the Enlightenment critique and reconsiders the force of this critique. Mitchell is quietly confident that this challenge can be met, without contesting the Enlightenment presupposition that religion must face criticism:

the restrictions placed on the exercise of reason by Hume and Kant are no longer appropriate to the scientific activity they were designed to fit, hence . . . once freed from these restrictions, reason can and should be restored to the domain of religion from which they and many of their successors sought to expel it. (82–3)

This point can be illustrated by the justly famous debate with Maurice Wiles over divine agency. Mitchell begins by inquiring as to why Wiles rejects the tenet of special revelation and is only willing to maintain general revelation. Wiles proposes that divine creativity is universal. A religion such as Christianity is defined by a specific, contingent and particular human response to this universally accessible general revelation.

Mitchell offers three assumptions as contributing explanations for the strong scepticism of Wiles:

1 the idea that special divine action is inherently in conflict with science;
2 biblical criticism has reinforced naturalism;
3 the employment of rather limited conceptions of divine inspiration.

He argues that all three assumptions are debatable. The first two points are matters of metaphysics or epistemology that are still open to debate. The intelligibility or coherence of special revelation at this level rests upon philosophical issues that cannot be said to be resolved, or even resolvable, to the benefit of the sceptic about special divine action. The cruder view of inspiration may be replaced by more subtle analogies, like that of the teacher–pupil relationship. He writes: 'There is not that sharp dichotomy between scientific explanation and other kinds of explanation which led so many nineteenth-century thinkers to dismiss rational theology as beyond redemption' (77). In this way Mitchell avoids also the disadvantage of the sharp dichotomy between the humanities and the natural sciences proposed by German thinkers such as Dilthey or Gadamer, while sharing with them the emphasis upon the necessary role of tradition, history, imagination and empathy in serious thought and the legitimacy of more informal forms of reasoning.

There is, Mitchell rightly argues, instead, a *continuum* of rational disciplines from physics and chemistry through the biological sciences to the humanities and metaphysics. Sainte-Beuve remarked that the origin of all discovery was to be 'amazed by what seems simple to the majority of mankind'. And it is clear that wonder can inspire the imagination both to operate creatively and also to illuminate the structures of reality. There is evidence of an aboriginal power of images summoned by scientific or poetic genius. We might consider Einstein's image of a rider of a beam of light carrying a mirror and his development of relativity theory or Kekulé's dream of the snake and his discovery of the benzene ring. Such examples of the role of creative imagination in the strict sense of ruminating on pregnant images in scientific discovery should discourage crude dichotomies, which are often lazily parasitic upon the nineteenth-century English coinage of 'science' as the distinct and superior domain of knowledge.

Yet the standard contrast between religion and science is usually attended by two misconceptions:

The first error consists in the conviction that scientific questions admit of a precise decision procedure whereas religious questions do not: scientific laws are certain, physical measurement is exact, and is there is a clearly marked boundary between scientific and ordinary thought. The first point was decisively challenged by Hume in his sceptical considerations about induction, the second by mistakes of observation. Furthermore, a botanist engaged in fieldwork employs his or her eyes to note colours, even if these are secondary qualities.[2]

The second error consists in the conviction that science deals with literal truth, religion with myth and metaphor. Like poetry it is a matter of how one feels – it has nothing to do with truth (78).

Mitchell observes:

To say that the human sciences and the humanities are inherently controversial is to recognise that, although a given position may in fact be rationally preferable to its rivals, this is rarely obvious . . . The issues in dispute are complex, highly ramified, and calling for trained judgement and sympathetic imagination. The resolution of any individual problem can rarely be achieved simply by inspecting the evidence provided by the present case. There will always be an immense background of theory, related to earlier observations, which cannot in practice be made wholly explicit, but which guides the thinking of the disputants. (25)

Mitchell is appealing to a notion of intuition in the sense of non-rigorous or informal reasoning.

Personal judgement and imaginative assent form part of a theory of rationality between the extremes of an exclusively rule-based conception of reasoning and a fideism which surrenders the claim of rationality to the hard sciences. I can only guess as to why the concept of imagination is not used. It may have suggested romantic arbitrariness. Ryle's urbanely expressed but crassly counterintuitive expulsion of mental images and, *a fortiori*, his wrong-headed theory of imagination as principally propositional pretending, seem to me to rival in sheer implausibility Norman Malcolm's claim that we do not have experiences in dreams.[3]

Imaginative context, tradition and the believer's reasons

Mitchell does write of the importance of the Romantic legacy:

That knowledge of God is not merely a matter of detached theoretical enquiry but rather of direct encounter is a truth that we should be grateful to receive from Schleiermacher and the Romantic movement, but it does not in the least follow from this insight that there is no need for philosophical enquiry. (83)

In this, Mitchell shows an elective affinity to Farrer in the first chapter, 'The Believer's Reasons', of *Faith and Speculation*. Farrer admits that 'there is no great mystery . . . about the source from which any given generation of believers derives the key-concepts of religion. It is to be found in tradition or history, not in a subliminal annex to the philosophy of cognition.'[4] Farrer is quite clear that faith is rarely *derived* from reasons or arguments, but is usually inherited from within a particular community of believers. The neutral approach to the grand question involves a fiction.[5] Nevertheless, he is profoundly conscious of the possibilities of delusion. Tradition must be tempered by the continual effort of interpretation and criticism. The believer may presume, if not assume, the rationality of faith. But that *presumption* of rationality must then be explored and tested.

Equally, however powerfully Mitchell defends the role of tradition and the importance of structures and institutions in human life, he strikingly refuses to reject the term 'liberal'. This makes for an obvious difference between Mitchell and, say, Gadamer or MacIntyre. The distinction Mitchell draws is that between prejudice and partiality. *Impartiality* does not imply neutrality (23). He uses the instance of the capacity to understand and learn from very different cultures, for instance of Aristotle making 'true and important' claims about ethics for us, as an instance of the possibility of genuine dialogue between radically different cultures. Mitchell pointedly uses the example of a discussion with a Hindu friend to reject the idea that we should infer from the lack of strictly neutral standards of rationality to the incommensurability of narratives (106). When considering genuine dialogue Mitchell observes that this depends not merely upon 'training but also upon natural endowments of empathy and imagination' (106). A further argument, employed by Mitchell, is based upon the capacity of traditions to evolve through criticism and responsiveness to facts.

There are great advantages to Mitchell's proposal. He can account easily for the intractable nature of disputes between theists and atheists. What is at stake is a complex world-view that cannot be articulated in strictly formal terms. Furthermore, Mitchell can do justice to the element of commitment that adherents can sustain, which explains the limits of a purely intellectual debate. Those who adhere to such a world-view show real tenacity in the face of criticism. Mitchell can give an account that does not reduce this to delusion or stupidity. Finally, he avoids the alternative of either an abstract natural theology or the appeal to faith. He neither limits Christian apologetics to a narrow rationalism nor immunizes it from critique.

> In so far as we have to act in the world, choices have to be made, and in so far as our actions have to be consistent, our choices need to be consistent too, that is to say they have to be based on some more or less coherent view of the world. Our choice of such a view of the world determines not only what we do, but also to a large extent, who we are. (37)

This is expounded further:

> Our conception of what it is to be a human being profoundly affects the way we treat people and the way we think we ought to treat them. There is, in fact, a reciprocal relationship between our intuitive judgements about people and our immediate responses to them and the more theoretical ideas about them that we have imbibed from our culture whether we are aware of them or not. (41)

Apparently unmediated responses to other agents are in fact parasitic upon tacit, or presupposed, theories or principles, or upon what one might call an imaginative view of the world. As far as I can tell, Mitchell tends to use the term 'intuition' to mean informal reasoning rather than immediate apprehension. It is precisely because Mitchell operates with a subtle picture of the mediating role of the cultural backdrop to *prima facie* immediate judgements that there is, at least implicitly, a strong role for the imagination in his thought, at least in the sense in which the French understand the idea of *l'imaginaire social*.[6]

In *Faith and Criticism* Mitchell uses the example of Freud in order to illustrate the significance of imaginative theoretical structures that contribute to our habitual perceptions and immediate judgements of other agents (41). But one could think of Marx as another example. It is sometimes naively supposed that Marx was describing capitalism, but there is little evidence of any field work in Manchester or the cotton mills. Marx was the classic case of the German professor employing the high road of the speculative *a priori*. The relevance of his theories to the world in which gigantic sums are won and lost between New York, London and Tokyo while we are asleep (perhaps half the GDP of the US economy) is even looser. Equally, one might reasonably harbour doubts as to the degree to which the interests and obsessions of those very sophisticated Viennese ladies on Freud's couch gave him hard and reliable scientific evidence into the universal human condition. Yet the imaginative impact of Freud and Marx as debunkers of fantasy upon twentieth-century intellectuals was pervasive. At one time in the last century in Cambridge it seems that a cocktail of Marxism and Freudianism was virtually a prerequisite for becoming a Head of House. Both these Victorian thinkers produced an imaginative vision of the human condition, and it was the power of this vision, rather than any empirical evidence that exerted such enormous influence.

Indeed, the pervasive nature of the theoretical ideas which 'we have imbibed from our culture' is evinced, as Mitchell observes, in those who 'venture into metaphysics without realising that this is what they are doing, and . . . claim scientific authority illicitly for their philosophical speculations' (28). The shaping force of the imagination can be seen in the way in which sociobiology takes up the metaphor of the struggle for survival.

Imaginative belief

An important point of contact between Farrer and Mitchell lies in the centrality of human personality for understanding God. In Farrer, this is an explicit metaphysical principle: the 'union of will with the primal Will'. The only God who can mean anything to the human mind is the God about whom the human will has something to do. Furthermore, the analogy between finite and infinite creativity is central for Farrer. Again, 'we know the action of a man can be the action of God in him'.[7] This is the paradigmatic instance of double agency'. Brian Hebblethwaite insists that Farrer speaks of the *paradox* – not the contradiction – of double agency. It appears paradoxical because of our inadequacies: 'we lack access to the "causal joint" of supernatural and the natural'.[8] Double agency is a paradox which 'arises simply as a by-product of the analogical imagination'.[9] Farrer uses the literary analogy of the author who 'has the wit to get a satisfying story out of the natural behaviour of the characters he conceives'. But though the source of divine action remains hidden, the effects are obvious.

It seems to me that the kind of apologetic or justification which Basil Mitchell mounts presupposes a vital connection between the soul's longing for God and the rationality of religious belief. Here is a sense of the 'vital connection' between religion and imagination: in that mysterious and inscrutable causal joint between human and divine activity:

> Our understanding of people, whose inexhaustibility entails that our knowledge of them is never final or complete, provides the closest analogy we have to our knowledge of God; and if it is true that it relies on a critical awareness of all sorts of signs and cues, as well as a defensible conception of what it is to be a human being, so must our awareness of God depend upon something comparable. (84)

On this model, the activity of the pupil does not exclude the initiative and the activity of the teacher. On the contrary, divine promising and forgiving are necessary to the model. Christian doctrine requires a concept of revelation and this depends upon the analogy of one person communicating to another truths about his character, purposes and intentions which that other person would not otherwise be in a position to know.[10] However, natural theology is insufficient to know God's purposes. God would have reason to communicate, and the Bible should be interpreted as God's self-revelation. The idea of communication presupposes some divine speech. For inspiration he uses the idea of a teacher inspiring a pupil.

One might pursue, by way of illustration, a passage in *Faith and Criticism* in which Mitchell discusses Jane Austen's *Emma*:

In the novel, Emma learns through her mistakes, and the process of learning is one in which she comes to see more clearly and judge more wisely in proportion as she is freed from self-centred pride. Her education is watched over by Knightley. (85)

Mitchell notes that, like the Romantics, Jane Austen was sensitive to the role of imagination and the will, and invoked Knightley's ability to 'imagine a range of different possible people that Emma might become and different choices she might make, and decide which one of them represents her real vocation' (86). He decides to trust her and by virtue of this he 'exerts his imagination to the full in order increasingly to understand her'. But Mitchell notes that if his judgement is to be well founded, his 'critical intellect' must also be really effective, if he wants to be sure that he understands her properly (86). Mitchell reasons further that despite starting with Christian revelation itself – and all that we are committed to by accepting it – there is no bar to the full exertion of our intellectual energies. Trust in a person, and even more so, trust in God, engages the emotions, the imagination, and the will, because it engages the whole person and, by that same token, engages the intellect as well. Faith is not so much opposed to knowledge as to vision. One recalls that Farrer uses St Paul on seeing through a glass darkly as the motto of *The Glass of Vision*. In that theological masterpiece Farrer gave us a fascinating and intriguing piece of intellectual biography, from which Basil Mitchell has already quoted a passage in the first chapter of this book:

> I had myself . . . been raised in a personalism which might satisfy the most ardent of Dr Buber's disciples. I thought of myself as set over against deity as one man faces another across a table, except that God was invisible and indefinitely great. And I hoped that he would signify his presence to me by way of colloquy; but neither out of the scripture I read nor in the prayers I tried to make did any mental voice address me. I believe at that time anything would have satisfied me, but nothing came: no 'other' stood beside me, no shadow of presence fell upon me. I owe my liberation from this *impasse*,

as far as I can remember, to reading Spinoza's *Ethics*. Those phrases which now strike me as so flat and sinister, so ultimately atheistic – *Deus sive Natura* (God, or call it Nature), *Deus, quatenus consideratur ut constituens essentiam humanae mentis* (God, in so far as he is considered the being of the human mind) – these phrases were to me light and liberation, not because I was or desired to be a pantheist, but because I could not find the wished-for colloquy with God.

Undoubtedly I misunderstood Spinoza, in somewhat the same fashion as (to quote a high example) St Augustine misunderstood Plotinus, turning him to Christian uses. Here, anyhow is what I took from Spinozism. I would no longer attempt, with the psalmist, 'to set God before my face'. I would see him as the underlying cause of my thinking, especially of those thoughts in which I tried to think of him. I would dare to hope that sometimes my thought would become diaphanous, so that there should be some perception of the divine cause shining through the created effect, as a deep pool, settling into clear tranquillity, permits us to see the spring in the bottom of it from which its waters rise. I would dare to hope that through a second cause the First Cause might be felt, when the second cause in question was a spirit, made in the image of the divine Spirit, and perpetually welling up out of his creative act.[11]

This remarkable passage echoes Coleridge's words in his *Biographia Literaria* about Spinoza as helping him keep alive 'the *heart* in the *head*' and thus to 'skirt, without crossing the sandy deserts of utter unbelief'.[12] It also gives us an important insight into Farrer's theology. Though Farrer does not employ the traditional scholastic method of cosmological inference from world to God, he clearly wishes to avoid the other extreme of the personalism in philosophy and theology of Martin Buber and Karl Barth. He writes (n.b. in 1948): 'when the Germans set their eyeballs and pronounce the terrific words "He speaks to thee" (*Er redet dich (sic) an*) . . . they are not speaking to my condition' says Farrer.[13] He is placing himself within the Platonic/Aristotelian tradition of which St Thomas is a good example. As such, he is allied to both the God of the philosophers and to the God of Abraham, Isaac and Jacob. This also explains why Farrer is at pains to insist upon the hierarchy of the mind: mankind is defined by the 'luminous apex of the mind' not the 'shadowy base'. *Pace* David Brown in his excellent article on Farrer 'God and Symbolic Action', I do not think we can say that Farrer is hostile to the creative role of the un or subconscious realm.[14] I think Farrer is making a point about anthropology. Man made in the image of God is *primarily* a rational creature.[15] This is the basic conviction lying behind the idea of 'a double personal agency in our one activity'.[16] God can act within and through finite human agents. Again, I think the target is the anthropological pessimism of Freud or Barth. Farrer is clearly standing in the tradition of natural theology and he wants a theory of inspiration as part of an account of divine action that coheres with his philosophical tenets, but the starting point for his natural theology is the experience of the believer – the fact of his own agency and the sense of his or her free and creative response to, and dependence upon God. He endeavours to use the principle of analogy based upon agency rather than a dialectical theology of the Word, but his metaphysics of analogy is based upon the necessarily inscrutable working of God. At one level God is necessarily hidden; at another he is evident to the imaginative eye of faith as it is *illuminated* by metaphysical reflection and *instructed* by revelation: 'Faith discerns not the images, but what the images signify: and yet we cannot discern it except through the images.'[17]

In this context, moreover, one might recall Farrer's employment of Gabriel Marcel's distinction between problems and mysteries. This is not to be confused with appeals to ignorance or the sacrifice of the intellect. Farrer accepts that we cannot articulate the facts of human personality; and yet we know these facts as realities. He thinks that metaphysics cannot be dispensed with. He argues that we have to distinguish the central problems of metaphysics, free will or the relation of the subject to the body, from scientific questions because natural science deals with specific *problems* relating to the specific questions and instruments of the inquiry. The results are real but 'highly abstract or selective'. On the other hand, philosophical puzzles depend upon the prior philosophical assumptions of any particular position. The relation of the active and the receptive intellect is a 'puzzle' for Aristotelians but not for behaviourists or Berkeleyans. God is a genuine *mystery* like free will or the nature of the self. Neither he nor they are open to scientific procedure, but they cannot be disposed of as factitious puzzles. Farrer sees the work of metaphysics as the 'sober criticism of images' that we can naturally employ to describe reality:

> The so-called problems of metaphysics are difficulties of description: that does not make them either unimportant, or easy to manage. On the contrary, they may be quite agonizing; nor are any questions of greater importance to a mind which desires to understand the nature of its real world. There is no finality about the description offered by metaphysics for the mysteries of existence, but there is advance in apprehension of the mysteries by the refining of the descriptions.[18]

The natural mystery which is the starting point of rational theology is the finite manifesting itself as the shadow of the infinite. Metaphysics is the description of natural mysteries by the criticism of analogies. And analogy is the name for 'sober and appropriate images'. Farrer's clear admiration for Aristotle should be allied to a certain scepticism towards the conceptual (e.g. *The Glass of Vision*, p. 45: 'the life of images, not of concepts').[19] The knowledge which literature and metaphysics can deliver is not to be confused with definitive articulation. This knowledge is, in a sense, experiential. I think it is clear from Farrer's excursion into the nature of metaphysical reasoning that he is concerned to do justice to the experiential component in metaphysics which eludes exhaustive definition: 'the soul does exist: there is nothing of which we are more aware, for it is we ourselves; only its uniqueness and singleness prevents our talking prose about it . . .'[20] Farrer employs the Platonic language of participation:

> [I]n our degree we all participate in supernatural act, for we do not receive revealed truth as simply a tale told about God

in the third person by others; we apprehend it as assured to us by God himself, or to put it otherwise, the description of divine mysteries ceases to be experienced by us as mere description: in the lines laid down by the description, the mysteries shine with their own light and presence; or rather with the light and presence of God.[21]

This is very close to the passage where he describes the liberating effect of Spinoza which helped him to think of the divine not as alien 'other', but rather as the 'underlying cause of my thinking'. So there might be a perception of the divine cause through the created effect.

But Farrer insists:

If we surrender metaphysical enquiry, we shall vainly invoke supernatural revelation to make up for our metaphysical loss of nerve. For if our cravenheartedness surrenders the ground of metaphysics, it will have surrendered the bridgehead which the supernatural liberator might land upon. Get a man to see the mysterious depth and seriousness of the act by which he and his neighbour exist, and he will have his eyes turned upon the bush in which the supernatural fire appears, and presently he will be prostrating himself with Moses, before him who thus names himself 'I am that I am'.[22]

The move here to Exodus 3.14 is very important. It was this passage, partly as a result of a strange translation of the Hebrew, that came to be read as God's own identifying himself with ultimate being.

Here we come back to the 'Barthian captivity' of a theology that refuses to mediate between revealed and natural truth. The organic model of revelation through the medium of the imagination is linked, however paradoxical this may seem, to Farrer's passionate defence of metaphysics. Although God is 'absolutely unique' we expect, he claims, religious mysteries:

to bear some analogy with natural realities because they are revealed in the stuff of human existence. So it seems that God's encounter with us must be a sort of encounter, analogous to our encounters with men; and that the parables or symbols through which God teaches us to imagine his action must be some sort of symbols parallel, perhaps, to the symbols of valid poetry.[23]

The point is really about divine agency rather than religious language. Farrer is not trying to translate talk of divine action into the merely figurative expression of a sense of deity, but to give an account of the status of talk about divine action. I think Farrer's theory that the 'stuff of inspiration is living images' is indebted to a certain legacy of Christian Romanticism. Farrer's stress upon the *organic* and *imaginative* nature of inspiration rather than the mechanical is very 'Romantic':

> But what springs up through wit and inspiration is not the gratuitous gift of the imagination to the intelligence: the previous labour of the intelligence is thrown down into the imagination as into a cauldron, from which it emerges again fused into new figures and, it may be, enriched with materials from the subconscious sphere, which were never in distinct consciousness at all . . . Such inspiration (always using the word in the secular sense) belongs to what is most godlike in the natural man: but it also belongs to what is most centrally human in him.[24]

Divine uniqueness, contemplation, joy and the mind's eye

There is another sense of imagination linked to the soul's longing for God. Austin Farrer shares with his great North African namesake, St Augustine, a concentration upon the unique nature of the soul:

> The soul is unique when compared with that which is not a soul; for if we are classifying created things, we must put soul all by itself on one side of the division, and on the other the whole host of things which the soul knows, loves, hates, feels, manages, copes with and exploits. But although the soul is unique by comparison with all that is not soul, it is in this

respect not unique, that there are many souls, yours and mine and the next man's, and these have a common nature, and I can know something about several such. But God is uniquely unique.[25]

I think that Farrer would have regarded the contemporary prevailing functionalist orthodoxy in the philosophy of mind, where the mind is seen in terms of information processing in the process of which a Martian, a computer or a human being might share an equivalent functional economy, as just as pernicious, flat and sinister as its cruder forebears in behaviourism and verificationism. God is a reality, immanent and active in all creatures through his continual creative power. And it is the soul that is the fountain of the creative imagination. But we could not speak of God even if we attain the vision of God – not for the Gnostic reason that God is radically and incommensurably beyond our apprehension, but for the solid Platonic/Aristotelian reason of divine uniqueness: 'It is his uniqueness and not only his hiddenness, which prevents our saying anything perfectly exact about him, except that he is himself.'[26]

Coleridge's reflections upon poetry were driven by a metaphysical conviction that a merely mechanical view of the mind as primarily associative, a view derived from Hobbes and Hume, could not explain the distinctive creative genius of a true poet like Wordsworth. This is in part the impact of the presence of Wordsworth as a companion, collaborator and friend, but it is more deeply motivated by the conviction that the creative dimension of the mind points to a level untouched by mechanical explanation.

All statements about God are enigmatic, like those of the soul. Farrer then faces an objection: is he not just reducing theology to poetry? Farrer's reply is that the metaphors of the poet illuminate if there is a real analogy between the items compared. The poet, however, is not worried about the accuracy of the analogy. In theology 'we must get behind the poetry to the real analogies'.[27] Farrer states at this point that personal analogies are best: God can be compared with human will and intellect but not with human passions. Farrer takes the example of the phrase 'the eternal spirit' as an example of this work by analogy. It expresses the paradoxical coincidence of living personality and the immutability of mathematical verity.

Part of Mitchell's argument must be about the capacity to see reality as a whole. The ability to do this is 'imaginative' – not in some pejorative and negative sense of 'phantasy'. The move from notional to imaginative assent to belief in God requires a disciplined imagination. In *Aids to Reflection*, Samuel Taylor Coleridge argued that: 'to believe and to understand are not diverse things, but the same thing in different periods of its growth. Belief is the seed, received into the will, of which the Understanding or Knowledge is the Flower, and the thing believed the fruit.'[28] Coleridge speaks of imagination as bringing the whole soul of man into activity. Mitchell is quite explicit about the role of the imagination in a total response to God. The poet, the lover and the theologian are, in Farrer's thought, of imagination quite compact. However, 'The lover and the poet at least look at something and see it'.[29] The theologian should endeavour to. Farrer goes on to insist that the 'great impediment to religion in this age' is the loss of the capacity to contemplate:

> No one ever looks at anything at all: not so as to contemplate it, to apprehend what it is to be that thing, and plumb, if he can, the deep fact of its individual existence. The mind rises from the knowledge of creatures to the knowledge of their creator, but this does not happen through the sort of knowledge which can analyse things into factors or manipulate them with technical skill or classify them into groups. It comes from the appreciation of things which we have when we love them and fill our minds and senses with them and feel something of the silent force and great mystery of their existence. For it is in this that the creative power is displayed of an existence higher and richer and more intense than all.[30]

Is this not 'joy' in the Wordsworth/Coleridgean sense?[31] The contemplative mood of 'joy' in Coleridge's poem 'Dejection' is explicitly linked to his 'shaping spirit of imagination'.[32] Or Ruskin exclaims: 'to see clearly is poetry, prophecy, and religion, – all in one'.[33] It is such imaginative moods that 'lift', as

Shelley puts it, 'the veil from the hidden beauty of the world'. The joy described by some of our greatest poets can be seen as the pinnacle of an imaginative component in cognition which is evident in mundane experience and extends up to very elevated experiences of the world as a coherent and purposive theatre of divine agency. One might think here of Coleridge's description of Wordsworth's poetry. Here 'objects observed', for which 'custom had bedimmed all the lustre' could be endowed with the 'depth and height of the ideal world'.[34] In such a way Coleridge muses that Wordsworth, in 'imaginative power', is closest to Shakespeare and Milton. Using Wordsworth's lines from 'Elegiac Stanzas, Suggested by a Picture of Peele Castle', Coleridge reflects upon Wordsworth. To employ his own words, which are at once an instance and an illustration, Wordsworth does indeed to all thoughts and to all objects:

> . . . add the gleam,
> The light that never was on sea or land,
> The consecration and the poet's dream.[35]

Such a paean to 'joy' can be misleading for us, especially since purely secular writers, such as Proust with his *moments bien-hereux* or Virginia Woolf, have accustomed us to imaginative epiphanies with no purely residual religious content. And many will associate Romantic epiphanies with pantheism. Yet I suspect that the concept of 'joy' is best understood as a name for the exalted mood of the contemplative liaison of the empirical eye and mind's eye by which the poet perceives items of sense experience as conveying, beyond themselves, the divine source.

To speak of the contemplative imagination is to reflect upon the relation of the empirical eye and what our great metaphysical bard William Shakespeare calls 'the mind's eye' (*Hamlet* I i 12). Wordsworth's power was primarily in this creative liaison of eye and mind's eye. And he was convinced that the poet's imaginative capacity is dependent upon the ability to penetrate truths obscured by the more narrow constraints of physical science and to envisage the hidden shape of reality. Here we are not so much talking of imagination in the sense of possession of mental images, the Kantian 'transcendental' power of the imagination, or of make-believe, but the imagination that enables the theist to see the world as real facts – discrete and apparently discordant and often grievously painful – and respect them as such, and at the same time to see these parts as belonging to a whole which one can affirm as grounded in a wholly good and transcendent God. This contemplative imagination is not the much-discussed capacity for 'seeing as' (whatever we see is seen *with the mind*) which is important, but the capacity to see *both x and y*. 'It is a capacity of the religious mind to see', as Coleridge observes, 'symbols: living *educts* of the imagination . . . consubstantial with the truths, of which they are the *conductors*', as opposed to the 'unenlivened, generalising Understanding'.[36] It is not that the religious mind fails to see the same objects in the world as the purely secular observer, since to see them in *exclusively* religious terms would be what the eighteenth century called rampant 'enthusiasm' or what we might designate madness. It is rather the sober capacity to see the same objects as *both* themselves *and* as conductors or symbols of another dimension of reality.

Atheism for Coleridge or Wordsworth can be construed as a failure of imagination. Through imagination the reality of certain *facts* can be experienced, and hence to emancipate the mind from what Coleridge calls 'the despotism of the eye'[37] and to be open to the impact of certain objects upon the soul. A Caspar David Friedrich landscape is a good instance of an appeal to both the empirical and the inner eye. His depictions have a certain realism and yet are aimed at an effect upon the soul rather than any purely visual experience. Milton is even more extreme. He writes:

Mine eyes be closed, but open left the cell of fancy
Of fancy, my internal sight.[38]

The blindness of the poet, whether Milton or Homer, is itself an image of the work of imagination. We are not mirrors of nature in any crude representational sense, and the Christian faith is a fidelity to the invisible causal joint of God and the soul, through the dark glass of our reason and imagination. The greatest poets explore and make articulate through images and analogies our often mute intimations of invisible reality, and I think Farrer's theological project is inextricably linked to this poetic and philosophical imagination.

Poetic truth

The exploration of the poetic within the canonical prophetic writings is largely a Romantic contribution to theology which goes back to another great Oxford divine, Robert Lowth. His *Sacred Poetry of the Hebrews* of 1753 discussed and analysed the poetic quality of the Hebrew prophetic writings. Farrer presents a fascinating account of how the lover, the theologian and the poet are all of an imagination compact in *The Glass of Vision*. But I wish to discuss in more detail Farrer's paper 'Poetic Truth' in the collection *Reflective Faith*. This is a discussion of the relation between poetry and theology and the use of metaphor in speaking of the soul and God: a great theme of the Romantics. Coleridge says that words are 'living powers, by which the things of most importance to mankind are actuated, combined and humanized'. Poets are transformers of the tongue. The poet diffuses a tone and spirit of unity that blends and (as it were) fuses. This fusing power of the poetic vision is in Farrer's mind when he draws analogies between poetical and prophetic inspiration: he speaks of 'this strange human passion for never saying what one means but always something else finds its most extreme and absolute development in the poets'.[39] What is the point of such bizarre convolution such as 'The curfew tolls the knell of parting day'. Why the use of metaphor? Is it mere drollery or relish of ingenuity? Sounding rather like John Ruskin, Farrer insists:

> the best figurative poetry speaks not to the frivolous intellect, but (if anything does) straight to the heart; and it does so better than plain prose. There seems then to be something which is better said with metaphor than without, which goes straighter to the mark by going crooked, and hits its aim exactly by flying at tangents. An odd fact, if true.[40]

Poetry, therefore, is not misrepresentation, as Bentham or Hume would insist, nor even ornament. It is *descriptive*. Farrer wants to attack two errors. One is that metaphor is the language of emotion. He makes the point that one can stir emotions often more effectively with literal language: 'A bull is charging you from behind' is more effective than talk of 'the playfellow of Europa'. Farrer distinguishes between two senses given to the words 'subjective' and 'feeling'. Poetry does express 'something subjective' and 'what is felt about things'. However, Farrer thinks it quite illegitimate to infer that poetry *only* tells us about the poet's emotions. He uses an analogy from the provincial (poorly lit) aquarium and the murky phenomena behind the glass with two observers: the philosopher (I think he means what we would usually call a 'scientist') and the poet. The first tries to distinguish the genuine fish from the distorting impact of the factors of light, glass, etc. The poet tries to describe the whole effect of the phenomenon of the fish in the tank in figurative language as a sea monster. The work of the poet is *descriptive*; but his domain of description is broader than that of the philosopher. 'The poet describes things just as he feels them, he does not describe what he feels *about* the things'.[41]

Coleridge proposes, in the famous chapter 13 'On the Imagination' of his *Biographia Literaria* that the imagination is a *tertium aliquid* or 'an inter-penetration of the counteracting powers, partaking of both' – that is, a middle point between subjective and objective.[42] Ultimately, Coleridge is trying to capture, I think, a similar insight about the nature of a poem as descriptive. Farrer distinguishes between the task of analysis and description. The scientist wishes to analyse the constituent elements of reality. The poet wishes to describe, '*to know what it is like*'. If a lover wants to describe his beloved, no scientific analysis of her skin will do. 'You will have to compare her skin to flowers.' Does the emotion blind or open the eyes of the lover? Farrer argues that it is reasonable to assume the latter. Perhaps the violence of passion can 'break down the dull custom of incomprehension, the blindness of the eyes and the hardness of heart'. 'It would be a strange fact if being passionately interested in something were always a bar to appreciating it truly.' This is a point that Burke and the Romantics (including Newman) made against the quasi-objectivity of 'sophisters, economists and calculators'. Knowledge is much more likely to be obtained if the mind is really committed and passionate about truth.[43] But this must mean a greater role for the emotions and imagination in the formation of belief than classical empiricism can concede.

Farrer writes:

> In poetic vision, then, and amatory passion, we are convinced that the object of our contemplation has a vividness of being, a distinctness of incommunicable individuality which scientific analysis would in vain hope to express – we are driven into metaphor. Science considers things in so far as they are the same; poetry, in so far as each is irreducibly itself. But what can we say about that which is truly unique.[44]

What is it like means 'What other thing does it resemble?' This is a question of analogies:

> All the unique creatures God has made resemble one another, at a greater or less distance; for all reflect in diverse manner or degree their one creator, and imitate his existence, as far as their lowliness allows, by being each themselves. But if they have family resemblance, they have an unlikeness too.[45]

Furthermore, Farrer insists, 'it is only by comparison and contrast with other things that we become aware of their individualities, and find out, as the saying is, what they are like'. Basil Mitchell has a telling argument against any exhaustive and exclusive dichotomy between the literal and the metaphorical. Drawing on Berkeley's distinction between metaphorical and proper analogy he argues that it is perfectly reasonable to apply concepts such as knowledge, faithfulness or love as attributes of the deity. This can be done in a manner which vastly exceeds our experience of these properties, while avoiding relegating these terms to mere metaphor. Stretched these concepts may be, but they express *literal* truths about God. Through a 'controlled exercise of imagination' by the use of proper analogy we can

develop a 'framework of theistic theory'.[46] Within such a context Farrer's claim that 'divine truth is supernaturally communicated to men in an act of inspired thinking which falls into
the shape of certain images' does not itself have to be regarded
as a metaphor that we are at a loss to interpret; for the language
of 'speaking' or 'communicating' in this context is an instance
of 'proper' rather than 'metaphorical analogy'. There is good
metaphysical precedence for this in one of the greatest poets.
When Dante speaks of the love moving the sun and the stars, it
would make a nonsense of his *Commedia* if that were just a
metaphor.

In *The Glass of Vision*, Farrer compares the post-Renaissance
poet with Jeremiah. Jeremiah, like Shakespeare, is a poet who
'sets images moving by musical incantation' and allows them to
arrange and express themselves as they 'ought'. But what is the
'ought' that constrains Jeremiah? The 'ought' that constrains
Shakespeare is not a metaphor. Farrer observes that there are
certain facts about human nature to which great poetry is
responsive. But Jeremiah is constrained by the impact of the will
of God upon his mind. 'He is not responding to the quality of
human life, he is responding to the demands of eternal will on
Israel as they make themselves heard in the determinate situation where he stands.'[47]

The difference between the two controlling pressures is
enormous. The scope of prophecy is much narrower than
poetry because of the 'elastic possibilities of human nature', and
the determinate nature of the divine will. The poet is a maker,
the prophet is a mouthpiece. But there is control in both cases.
Poetry is a technique of divination, Farrer insists: it is *in* the
poetic process that the prophet receives his message.

> Whatever signs or omens set the incantation of shapely words
> moving in the prophet's mind, it went on moving and form-
> ing itself with a felt inevitability, like that of a rhapsodical
> poetry which allows for no second thoughts: it formed itself
> under a pressure or control which the prophet experienced
> as no self-chosen direction of his own thinking, but as the
> constraint of the divine will.[48]

Here we can see a clear instance of Farrer's theory of *double agency*. The emphasis is upon the organic and vital nature of the process. The great images are 'alive and moving', 'vital images'. Farrer writes:

When I think of God as addressing man in revelation, I naturally fall into the same posture and become the victim of my parable. If you address me you are outside me; so, then, I suppose, is God. But then, on serious reflection, none of us can really maintain this. God is no more outside me than within; I am his creation just as much as you are, or as the physical world is. He has the secret key of entry into all his creatures; he can conjoin the action of any of them with his will in such fashion as to reveal himself specially through them. God speaks without and within; he reveals himself both through the situation with which he presents the recipients of revelation, and through the imagination, in terms of which he leads them to see and hear the voices and the sights surrounding them. How should it – how could it – be otherwise? The process is gradual; God has employed, he has not forced, the action of his creatures; he teaches us also to discern revelation from revelation and see where the flower and fruit borne by the branching plant of sacred truth are to be found.[49]

Furthermore, Farrer notes that 'from the fact that the craftsman is preparing materials you may guess that he is about some work, but it may be impossible for men or angels to infer what the work is to be without communication with the craftsman's mind'.[50] And it is the whole point of Farrer's typological analysis of St Mark's Gospel that 'The act of God always overthrows human expectation: the Cross defeats our hope: the Resurrection terrifies our despair.'[51] Yet Farrer's emphasis is upon continuity between inspiration poetic and divine rather than the gulf. It is by means of the images which are 'implanted' that revelation 'grows', images that 'in growing, are transformed, they grow out fresh branches, they fertilize neighbouring and as yet purely natural imaginations'.[52] Farrer presents us with a metaphysics of the imagination.[53]

Conclusion

In his illuminating essay, 'The Place of Symbols in Christianity', Basil Mitchell describes the oscillation within the Christian tradition between an insistence upon the inadequacy of images or symbols (the negative or mystical way) and an excessive credulity in images (idolatry). Yet he observes:

> Philosophically speaking, I believe that we are in a better position now than for a very long time to maintain a proper balance between these two tendencies, the apophatic and the anthropomorphic. We are now much more aware of the essential part played by the imagination in all creative thought, not excluding natural science, and also of the mysteriousness of personal life.[54]

Farrer, too, emphasizes that:

> the excellence of mind consists of conscious intelligence, but of a conscious intelligence based always on acute senses and riding upon a vigorous imagination. For although the excellence of mind is an act of thinking, the act of thinking is not self-sufficient, but has constant recourse to the imagination; and out of such recourse wit and (in the secular sense) inspiration arise.[55]

Farrer is explicitly repudiating any crass opposition between reason and imagination. He uses the image of the cauldron to describe the fusing activity of imagination as distinct from mechanical patterns of association. And he is also pointing to the importance of imagination in touching those levels of mind that lie beneath consciousness. The imagination is:

> a sort of focus into which is drawn together much that seems to us most important in the common essence of our human existence. The phrase which is just right has infinite overtones: or it awakens echoes in all the hidden caves of our minds.[56]

Farrer's suggestion can be put like this: Do we follow the path of so much twentieth-century philosophy and give up metaphysics and philosophical theology as the product of the bewitching capacity of language to hypostatize practices and dispositions as substances and entities, and proceed, like the wily Ulysses, to withstand these sirens and purge our concepts of folk and theological leaven? Or, is it conceivable that our language can reasonably strain to express facts and phenomena that are real but genuinely puzzling and which resist exhaustive conceptual articulation? Perhaps, ultimately, only images suffice to express some of these mysterious realities. Such is Farrer's claim: 'the stuff of inspiration is living images'.

It is the great virtue, I believe, of both Austin Farrer and Basil Mitchell to have defended a vision of theology in which the continuum of human creativity and divine action is so ably asserted. Why does this emphasis upon the creation of human and divine freedom and creativity matter? A century ago the great German sociologist Max Weber gave an oration to young scholars, *Wissenschaft als Beruf*.[57] He observed that the modern world is one of re-emergent polytheism. The beautiful, the true – to say nothing of the good – have no overarching unity in contemporary culture. The legacy of this is a science stripped of values, art devoid of beauty, ethics divorced from truth, a milieu in which the very idea of the human person in God's world seems at best quaint and anachronistic, at worst simply incoherent and erroneous. This was for the Romantics a debilitating legacy of the Enlightenment, and was eloquently excoriated by Coleridge, who was particularly fond of the biblical adage: 'WHERE NO VISION IS, THE PEOPLE PERISHETH'. But theological positivism as a reaction merely reinforces the malaise and becomes itself a variant of Gnosticism. The thinking of Austin Farrer and Basil Mitchell constitutes a rich, subtle, and imaginative articulation of the relation of faith and criticism, religious belief and rational justification. We can be particularly grateful for the shaping spirit of Farrer's vision.[58]

Notes

1 Basil Mitchell, *Faith and Criticism*, Oxford: Clarendon Press 1994, p. 76. Further page references in the text are from this book.

2 Harold Jeffreys, *Scientific Inference*, Cambridge: Cambridge University Press 1931, p. 183. I am very grateful to George Watson for pointing me to this work.

3 G. Ryle, *The Concept of Mind*, London: Penguin Books 1949, pp. 232–63; Norman Malcolm, *Dreaming*, London: Routledge and Kegan Paul 1976.

4 Austin Farrer, *Faith and Speculation: An Essay in Philosophical Theology*, London: A. & C. Black 1967, p. 4.

5 Ibid., p. 2.

6 See Charles Taylor, *Modern Social Imaginaries*, Durham NC and London: Duke University Press 2004.

7 *Faith and Speculation*, p. 66.

8 Brian Hebblethwaite, *Philosophical Theology and Christian Doctrine*, Oxford: Blackwell 2005, p. 140.

9 *Faith and Speculation*, p. 66.

10 See Basil Mitchell, *The Justification of Religious Belief*, London: Macmillan 1973, p. 145.

11 Austin Farrer, *The Glass of Vision*, London: Dacre Press 1948, pp. 7f.

12 Samuel Taylor Coleridge, *Biographia Literaria* I, London: Routledge 1983, p. 152.

13 *The Glass of Vision*, p. 8.

14 David Brown, 'God and Symbolic Action', in Brian Hebblethwaite and Edward Henderson (eds), *Divine Action: Studies Inspired by the Philosophical Theology of Austin Farrer*, Edinburgh: T & T Clark 1990, pp. 103–22.

15 *Faith and Speculation*, p. 50.

16 *The Glass of Vision*, p. 33.

17 Ibid., p. 110.

18 Ibid., p. 63.

19 The same applies to Farrer's 'Thomism'. His debt to Aquinas is huge, his affinity to the textbook neo-Thomism of his contemporaries slender.

20 Austin Farrer, *Reflective Faith: Essays in Philosophical Theology* (ed. Charles C. Conti), London: SPCK 1972, p. 34.

21 *The Glass of Vision*, p. 32.

22 Ibid., p. 78.

23 Austin Farrer, *Interpretation and Belief* (ed. Charles C. Conti), London: SPCK 1976, p. 45.

24 *The Glass of Vision*, pp. 24–6.

25 *Reflective Faith*, pp. 34f.

26 Ibid., p. 35. Compare Thomas Aquinas, *Summa Theologiae* Ia. 3 on divine simplicity: God is not a member of a series, and this claim about God 'in himself' is decisive for questions 12 and 13 of the *Summa* about how we know or speak about God. I am grateful to Denys Turner for pointing this out to me.

27 *Reflective Faith*, p. 36.

28 Samuel Taylor Coleridge, *Aids to Reflection* (ed. John Beer), London: Routledge 1993, p. 194.

29 *Reflective Faith*, p. 37.

30 Ibid., pp. 37f.

31 One might compare Farrer with Coleridge: 'Hast thou ever raised thy mind to the consideration of EXISTENCE, in and by itself, as the mere act of Existing? Hast thou ever said to thyself thoughtfully, IT IS! Heedless in that moment, whether it were a man before thee, or a flower, or a grain of sand?.' *The Friend* I, London: Routledge 1969, p. 514.

32 S. T. Coleridge, *Poems* (ed. John Beer), London: Dent 1986, pp. 280–3.

33 John Ruskin, 'Modern Painters' in *The Works of John Ruskin* (ed. E. T. Cook and Alexander Wedderburn), London: George Allen 1903–12, V, p. 177.

34 *Biographia Literaria* I, p. 80.

35 Ibid., vol. II p. 151.

36 S. T. Coleridge, *Lay Sermons* (ed. R. J. White), London: Routledge 1972, pp. 28–9.

37 *Biographia Literaria* I, p. 107.

38 John Milton, *Paradise Lost*, VIII, 461.

39 *Reflective Faith*, p. 24.

40 Ibid., p. 25.

41 Ibid., p. 49.

42 *Biographia Literaria* I, p. 300. Coleridge is rather elliptical in this passage, but this is how I interpret him.

43 Edmund Burke, *Reflections on the French Revolution* (1790), London: Dent [1910], p. 73.

44 *Reflective Faith*, p. 31.

45 Ibid., p. 32.

46 Basil Mitchell, *How to Play Theological Ping-Pong: Collected Essays on Faith and Reason*, London: Hodder & Stoughton 1990, p. 193.

47 *The Glass of Vision*, pp. 126f.

48 Ibid., pp. 128f.

49 *Interpretation and Belief*, p. 44.

50 *The Glass of Vision*, p. 30.

51 Ibid., p. 139.

52 Ibid., p. 136.
53 See Ingolf Dalferth's critical but illuminating essay 'Esse Est Operari. The Anti-Scholastic Theologies of Farrer and Luther', *Modern Theology* 1 (1985), pp. 183–211.
54 *How to Play Theological Ping-Pong*, p. 189.
55 *The Glass of Vision*, p. 24.
56 Ibid., p. 119.
57 Max Weber, 'Wissenschaft als Beruf', in W. J. Mommsen and W. Schluchter with B. Morgenbrod (eds), *Max Weber, Gesamtausgbe*, München: Mohr/Siebeck 1992, pp. 99–101.
58 I wish to thank Mark Wynn, Dave Leal, Tim Mawson, Chris Insole and Denys Turner for helpful suggestions. I have a special debt to Brian Hebblethwaite for detailed comments and to both Basil Mitchell and Ann Loades for their help and encouragement.

Appendix

Sermon preached by the Rt Revd Richard Harries, Bishop of Oxford, at Oriel College, Oxford on 8 September 2004

Austin Farrer was a modest man and I do not think he would have appreciated hagiography on an occasion like this. This conference, and our presence here this evening, is witness enough to the very high regard in which we continue to hold him. What I want to do is reflect on some of the ways in which his legacy is still crucially important for us today. I am not thinking so much of his major scholarly works and insights, which have been considered in papers and discussion at this conference, but of Farrer as a communicator of the Christian faith, especially in his more accessible writings and sermons.

I take five qualities or characteristics which are as essential today as they were in his time for a church which wants to be serious about communicating what the first Christians called good news.

First, his acute but totally unpretentious sensitivity to the intellectual and moral currents and questions of the age. The sermons are deceptive in this as in other matters. They can seem simple, even chatty and homely and they are always biblical and devotional. But the first reason that they spoke to people then is that they addressed, in however hidden a way, some question or questions that people were beginning to articulate in their minds. There was absolutely no display about this. As we know there was no reference to books, public controversies, academic issues and so on. But in almost every paragraph Farrer addressed some real difficulty which people were beginning to feel; not just intellectual difficulties but, perhaps even more important, moral and psychological ones. The second reading from Farrer this evening, for example, takes the question of power and the feeling that however benignly conceived God's power might be, this was experienced by us humans as oppressive. 'The universal misuse of human power has the sad effect that power, however lovingly used, is hated.' I believe that underneath the philosophical difficulties which many people have about the Christian faith there is often to be found a negative reaction that is at once moral and emotional and the Church is still much too reluctant to face such feelings. They were, however, often there as part of the unspoken background to Austin Farrer's sermons.

Second, there was his capacity for sustained, probing and accurate analysis. He subjected Christian ideas and phrases to precise, minute examination in order to show what might or might not be valid about them. Of the many examples one could take I point to the line in Mrs Alexander's famous hymn 'There was no other good enough to pay the price of sin', which he subjected to a six-page examination: accepting the line as parable or metaphor he tried to bring out what it could and could not legitimately suggest about Christ's saving death. Here and elsewhere it was thought at its most rigorous, except that word gives the wrong impression about the style of what emerged from his sustained concentration. The thought was rigorous but the style was relaxed. I like the description of his method of working recorded by his wife. He would sit down totally absorbed in thought for an hour or so and then jump up with the words 'I think I will write that one down'. It was this combination of sensitivity to the intellectual questions of his time, together with his capacity for sustained, concentrated, intellectual analysis that produced sermons about which C. S. Lewis wrote, 'In each of them there is matter out of which some theologians would have made a whole book'.

Third, and this may seem more surprising, his thought was always tested out in his own actual experience. The 1960s were the time of Harry Williams, telling us to be true to ourselves. It was the time when D. H. Lawrence was at the height of his popularity. Two people apparently a world away from Austin Farrer. You certainly can't imagine him telling us to be true to our own experience: but that's precisely what he was in his own case. I think of his own understanding of faith as something that gets into our heart and mind even before we begin to probe the intellectual questions about it. I think of the moving yet unsentimental sermons referring to his Baptist father and to his mother, their love for him and their own ardent faith. Then there is the famous passage in his 1948 Bampton lectures, published as *The Glass of Vision* to which Basil Mitchell has already referred but like so many of Austin Farrer's good things, well bears repetition. He said that he had been 'reared in a personalism which might satisfy the most ardent of Dr Buber's disciples' but he simply found it unreal. So,

> when Germans set their eyeballs and pronounce the terrific words 'He speaks to thee' I am sure, indeed, that they are saying something, but I am still more sure that they are not speaking to my condition.

He said he was liberated from this by reading Spinoza:

> I would no longer attempt, with the Psalmists, 'to set God before my face'. I would see him as the underlying cause of my thinking, especially those thoughts in which I tried to think of him. I would dare to hope that sometimes my thought would become diaphanous . . .

Then there is his friend Philip at college, with whom he spent three years as quite a close acquaintance, but who committed suicide. He drew painful lessons from this both for himself and us.

> It is not much use in such a case praying for people if your prayer consists in telling God to make them good Christians. We should do better, if we were telling God all the good and delightful qualities he has put into our friend, and were thanking him for them with all sincerity. When you have blessed God for your friend, you can go on to pray for his blessing by God. This is the sort of prayer that breaks down barriers.

D. H. Lawrence wrote a poem called 'Thought' in which he wrote:

> Thought, I love thought
> But not the jiggling and twisting of already
> existent ideas
> I despise that self-important game.

He went on to say that

> Thought is the testing of statements on the
> touchstone of the conscience,
> Thought is gazing on to the face of life, and reading what can
> be read
> Thought is pondering over experience, and coming to a con-
> clusion.
> Thought is not a trick, or an exercise, or a set of dodges,
> Thought is a man in his wholeness, wholly attending.

I believe Austin Farrer passed that D. H. Lawrence test.

Fourth, his intellectual endeavours were never separated from his spiritual life. As he put it 'We know on our knees'. The result was that he was an extraordinarily unified person. As Basil Mitchell has put it: 'There was no discernible difference of tone between preaching and lecturing or between lecturing and everyday speech.' The first reading from Farrer this evening said:

> After all the detection of shams, the clarification of argument, and the sifting of evidence – after all criticism, all analysis – a man must make up his mind what there is most worthy of love, and most binding on conduct, in the world of real exist-ence. It is this decision, or that discovery that is the supreme exercise of truth seeking intelligence.

When I was at Cuddesdon there were two sets of lectures that made the whole experience of college worthwhile. One was by Bill Vanstone; the other was the series of Holy Week lectures by Austin Farrer. He came quietly and quickly up the aisle at

Cuddesdon parish church, mounted the pulpit and without any ado talked to God for an hour before descending the pulpit and walking quickly out again with as little fuss as he had come in. It was a privilege to overhear him talking to God. I also came out of the church with a sense that as he had spoken my mind had gone click, click, click as question after scarcely formulated question seemed to receive an answer and a fresh insight. I would have been hard put to decide whether it was a spiritual experience or an intellectual treat. It was of course both. And this highlights the nature of Farrer's genius. Genius normally consists of one talent in extreme degree. Farrer's was of three aspects, the mind, the imagination and the spirit, fused together in such a way that each reached its perfection in relation to the other two.

Fifth, he knew that human words, though we have to use them, were as misleading as leading, in their attempts to point us to God. Images had to be broken then remade, then broken and remade again and again. This was because that which he sought to convey ultimately eludes any attempt we might make to grasp and possess. He would have agreed with his Oxford contemporary, G. B. Caird that 'We must know God or perish. But unless we know God as ultimate mystery we do not know him at all.' What Leslie Houlden has described as the poetry in his sermons, served a very specific theological purpose. It wasn't just there to move us. It was there to indicate that the reality with which we deal is beyond our stammering human words.

Austin Farrer was a passionate believer in the fact that this life has its consummation beyond space and time, in the endlessness of God and our delight in him. He could not understand how Christians could sit light to that belief. So, in this hope which he so much made his own, we remember him. In one sermon he said

> I knew a man whose name, though uncanonised, I shall always silently mention when I recall at the altar of God those saints whose fellowship gives reality to our prayers . . . Man knows God only by yielding to him; we do not know the fountain of our being, so long as we are occupied in by stop-

ping it with mud. So the saint is our evidence, and other men, of course, for the glimpses of sanctity that are in them.

So we thank God for Austin Farrer, a continuing inspiration both through his writings and his unified person, in whom mind and spirit and imagination were gathered together in a single focus; one who was indeed diaphanous to the ground of our being and the goal of our longing, to whom, Father, Son and Holy Spirit, be all glory, now and forever. Amen.

Select Bibliography

Works by Farrer referred to in this book

Monographs

Finite and Infinite, London: Dacre Press 1943, 2nd edn 1959.
The Glass of Vision, London: Dacre Press 1948.
A Rebirth of Images: The Making of St John's Apocalypse, London: Dacre Press 1949.
A Study in St Mark, London: Dacre Press 1951.
St Matthew and St Mark, London: Dacre Press 1954.
The Freedom of the Will, London: A. & C. Black 1958.
Love Almighty and Ills Unlimited: An Essay on Providence and Evil, London: Collins 1962.
The Revelation of St John the Divine, Oxford: Clarendon Press 1964.
Saving Belief: A Discussion of Essentials, London: Hodder & Stoughton 1964.
A Science of God?, London: Geoffrey Bles 1966.
Faith and Speculation: An Essay in Philosophical Theology, London: Adam & Charles Black 1967.

Collections

Reflective Faith: Essays in Philosophical Theology (edited by Charles C. Conti), London: SPCK 1972.
Interpretation and Belief (ed. Charles C. Conti), London: SPCK 1976.

Sermons

Said or Sung: An Arrangement of Homily and Verse, London: The Faith Press 1960.
A Celebration of Faith, London: Hodder and Stoughton 1970.
The End of Man, London: SPCK 1973.
The Brink of Mystery, London: SPCK 1976.

Select Bibliography

Secondary Literature

Books

Conti, Charles, *Metaphysical Personalism*, Oxford: Oxford University Press 1995.

Curtis, Philip, *A Hawk among Sparrows: A Biography of Austin Farrer*, London: SPCK 1985.

Eaton, Jeffrey C., *The Logic of Theism*, Lanham MD: University Press of America 1981.

Eaton, Jeffrey C. and Loades, Ann (eds), *For God and Clarity: New Essays in Honor of Austin Farrer*, Allison Park PA: Pickwick Publications 1983.

Hebblethwaite, Brian and Henderson, Edward (eds), *Divine Action: Essays Inspired by the Philosophical Theology of Austin Farrer*, Edinburgh: T & T Clark 1990.

Hefling, Charles C., *Jacob's Ladder: Theology and Spirituality in the Thought of Austin Farrer*, Cambridge MA: Cowley Publications 1979.

Hein, David and Henderson, Edward Hugh, *Captured by the Crucified: The Practical Theology of Austin Farrer*, New York/London: T & T Clark International 2004.

Loades, Ann and McLain, Michael (eds), *Hermeneutics, the Bible and Literary Criticism*, New York: St Martin's Press 1992.

McLain, F. Michael and Richardson, W. Mark, *Human and Divine Agency: Anglican, Catholic and Lutheran Perspectives*, Lanham: University Press of America 1999.

Articles

Brümmer, Vincent, 'Farrer, Wiles and the Causal Joint', *Modern Theology* 8 (1992), pp. 1–14.

Curtis, Philip, 'The Rational Theology of Dr Farrer', *Theology* 73 (1970), pp. 249–56.

Dalferth, Ingolf, '*Esse Est Operari*: The Anti-Scholastic Theologies of Farrer and Luther', *Modern Theology* 3 (1985), pp. 183–210.

Eaton, Jeffrey C., 'The Problem of Miracles and the Paradox of Double Agency', *Modern Theology* 1 (1984/5), pp. 211–22.

Emmet, Dorothy et al., 'Review Discussion of Dr Farrer's *A Science of God?*', *Theoria to Theory* 1 (1966), pp. 55–9.

Glasse, John, 'Doing Theology Metaphysically', *Harvard Theological Review* 59 (1966), pp. 319–50.

Hebblethwaite, Brian, 'Austin Farrer's Concept of Divine Providence', *Theology* 73 (1970), pp. 541–51.

Select Bibliography

Henderson, Edward Hugh, 'Valuing in Knowing God: An Interpretation of Austin Farrer's Religious Epistemology', *Modern Theology* 3 (1985), pp. 165–82.

Morris, Jeremy N., 'Religious Experience in the Philosophical Theology of Austin Farrer', *Journal of Theological Studies*, n.s 45 (1994), pp. 569–92.

Platten, Stephen, 'Diaphanous Thought: Spirituality and Theology in the Work of Austin Farrer', *Anglican Theological Review* 69 (1987), pp. 30–50.

Wiles, Maurice, 'Farrer's Concept of Double Agency', *Theology* 84 (1981), pp. 243–9.

Wilson, William McF., 'A Different Method, a Different Case: The Theological Program of Julian Hartt and Austin Farrer', *The Thomist* 53 (1989), pp. 599–633.

Index

Index